So You Think You Can Spell?

So You Think You Can Spell?

*

Killer Quizzes for the
Incurably Competitive and
Overly Confident

David L. Grambs and Ellen S. Levine

A Perigee Book

A PERIGEE BOOK
Published by the Penguin Group
Penguin Group (USA) Inc.
375 Hudson Street, New York, New York 10014, USA
Penguin Group (Canada), 90 Eglinton Avenue East, Suite 700, Toronto, Ontario M4P 2Y3,
Canada (a division of Pearson Penguin Canada Inc.) • Penguin Books Ltd., 80 Strand, London
WC2R 0RL, England • Penguin Group Ireland, 25 St. Stephen's Green, Dublin 2, Ireland
(a division of Penguin Books Ltd.) • Penguin Group (Australia), 250 Camberwell Road,
Camberwell, Victoria 3124, Australia (a division of Pearson Australia Group Pty. Ltd.) •
Penguin Books India Pvt. Ltd., 11 Community Centre, Panchsheel Park, New Delhi—110 017,
India • Penguin Group (NZ), 67 Apollo Drive, Rosedale, North Shore 0632, New Zealand
(a division of Pearson New Zealand Ltd.) • Penguin Books (South Africa) (Pty.) Ltd.,
24 Sturdee Avenue, Rosebank, Johannesburg 2196, South Africa

Penguin Books Ltd., Registered Offices: 80 Strand, London WC2R 0RL, England

While the author has made every effort to provide accurate telephone numbers and Internet
addresses at the time of publication, neither the publisher nor the author assumes any responsibility for errors, or for changes that occur after publication. Further, the publisher does not have
any control over and does not assume any responsibility for author or third-party websites or their
content.

First edition: October 2009

Library of Congress Cataloging-in-Publication Data

So you think you can spell? : killer quizzes for the incurably competitive and overly confident /
David L. Grambs and Ellen S. Levine.— 1st ed.
    p. cm.
  ISBN 978-0-399-53528-4
  1. Spellers.   2. English language—Orthography and spelling—Problems, exercises, etc.
3. English language—Orthography and spelling—Juvenile literature.   I. Grambs, David.
II. Levine, Ellen.
  PE1145.2.S6 2009
  428.1'3—dc22   2009022407

PRINTED IN THE UNITED STATES OF AMERICA

10 9 8 7 6 5 4 3 2 1

Most Perigee books are available at special quantity discounts for bulk purchases for sales promo-
tions, premiums, fund-raising, or educational use. Special books, or book excerpts, can also be
created to fit specific needs. For details, write: Special Markets, Penguin Group (USA) Inc., 375
Hudson Street, New York, New York 10014.

In memory of Abe Chait,
Ted Able, and Jim Chatfield

Contents

Introduction

When was the last time you took a spelling test or competed in a bee?

Would you say your confidence in your spelling is at best faith-based?

From *abacus* to *zyzzyva*, our word-rich but irrational, irregular, and often bamboozling English language offers no spelling rules that are absolute or trustworthy. As you're probably aware, there are exceptions galore when it comes to spelling rules—far too many of them to prove the rule. Thus the orthography of English continues to be frustrating and troublesome.

Perfect, that is, for devising hard, harder, and heartless spelling tests, quizzes, and bees.

So You Think You Can Spell? is a self-contained spelling adventure for the individual of any age. No classrooms, teachers, hosts, word pronouncers, or judges necessary. No spell-check here. Just an opportunity for a reality check. Put yourself to the test!

This is a book for fairly good, very good, and exceptional spellers, or those who wish to be; and for any well-read person or ever-curious reader who has a broadly knowledgeable, if not always working or eloquently employed, acquaintanceship with many English words.

To be a good speller is to a considerable degree to have a good vocabulary—to be on good terms with English, to be good on terms.

We also hope this book catches the eye of the thousands of adult spelling bee aficionados across the country, whether to help keep one orthographically in shape or as an inspiration for creating one's very own spelling bee. (See "Planning a Bee—Some Tips," page 268.)

Increasing your vocabulary, even while you're improving your spelling, is nothing to be sniffed at. It's sometimes called word power. You're bound to come up against words (and their definitions) in these pages that you don't know. But you'll acquire them for yourself through these encounters.

What can count most here in how well one does on many and various spelling challenges are some sound early education; past exposure to and enjoyment of books, periodicals, and the electronic media; a temperament that likes to get even little things right; and at least a touch of *sprachgefühl*, or feeling for words—not your basic gray-matter smarts or tested IQ score. (Nobody has as yet found any significant correlation between being able to spell *thalassocracy*, *paillasse*, and *salchow* and individual intelligence, and you probably know or know of brilliant scientists, artists, or writers who were or are hopeless spellers.)

Knowing a little French, Italian, Spanish, or classical Greek or Latin won't hurt, either, as you'll see in taking these tests. English, and the best English, often has a very strong foreign accent.

While many people *are* actually good spellers, many more think they are, a bit smugly if not hubristically or delusionally. This book may have some unpleasant surprises in store for them. Spelling tends to be an utter disrespecter of the factors of age, gender, diplomas, professional titles, haughty accents, and literary or literati snobbery. Again, the well-read are not always the well-spelled.

Not too long ago, a random survey of 2,500 people between the ages of eighteen and sixty by WhiteSmoke (a company specializing in writing and grammar software) found that 40 percent of them could not pick out, from three choices, the correct spelling of *questionnaire*. Many were poor spellers, yet ("despite their dismal spelling ability") nearly a third of the respondents reckoned their spelling was excellent and another 46 percent claimed it was good. (*So You Think You Can Spell?* will make a thoughtfully ameliorative, edifying gift for such mistakenly confident individuals—and they will be the better for it.)

In a nutshell, English spelling has countless *idiosyncracies*—one of them being the correct spelling of that word: it's *idiosyncrasies*.

But disspelling the problem of mispelling in our great English language is not properly possible. Not properly because it's *dispelling*, to be correct, not *disspelling*, and it's *misspelling*, not *mispelling*.

On the other hand, one could argue that a single spelling error is not exactly sacreligious. Rather, it's—exactly—*sacrilegious*.

Forgive us, but did you, or didn't you, notice the misspellings above immediately?

English spelling continues to be not only provocative but provoking. This book (you might note on your gift card) celebrates the quintessential quirks, quotidian questions, quizzical quandaries, querulous quibbles, qualmish queries, quarrelsome qualifications, quixotic quiddities, and queer quavering quagmire of that provocative and provoking language: English as she is writ.

About the Tests

Answers for all tests are provided at the back. (Peekers may have points deducted from their score.)

In some cases, two or more spellings are acknowledged as correct. Variant or alternative spellings are noted in dictionaries as being acceptable, whether "equal" in validity and usage or only as a secondary choice. But dictionaries differ in this regard, and many "also" spellings are at best dubious.

Most test formats in *So You Think You Can Spell?* include brief definitions (which always appear within parentheses). Where there is no definition, you'll be pretty likely to know the word's meaning.

Pronunciations—only one is supplied—are in the form of sound-approximating syllables (or SIL-uh-buls), with the stressed syllable in capital letters.

This commonly used phonetics style is admittedly simplistic and improvisatory when it comes to nuances of spoken English. But for the purposes of this book, we think, this system does the job. It spares the reader from having to deal with and interpret those tiny symbol squiggles, or abstruse diacritics, that only lexicographers and linguists feel comfortable with; or from having to refer constantly to one of those "pronunciation key" boxes sometimes found in dictionaries at the bottom of a page.

You'll notice that these syllabled phonetics sometimes seem to be precisely what you suspect the correct spelling is. Do they "give it away"? Maybe. Maybe not. You don't want to jump too quickly to the RAWNG conclusion.

Formats and Types of Tests

Formats vary throughout, as do the lengths of the challenges (in number of words to be spelled, that is). You'll find tests of ten words, and of fifteen, twenty, twenty-five, thirty, and fifty words. Even of three and five words (see "Quizzicles, Fluster Clusters, and Killer Bees," page 8).

Some of the challenges focus unsparingly on thorny bugaboos that plague people when they write—like those -able or -ible dilemmas that so many of us wish would just go away.

There are initial warm-up tests, and there are tests on parts of words (both middles and endings); on words that may or may not have a doubled consonant; on one-syllable words; on (foreign) loan words for which you must provide accent (or diacritical) marks where appropriate; on terms that are written as either one word or two (which?); on words to be matched with their correct definition; on the odd, less familiar plurals of certain words; on words whose letters have been scrambled . . .

If you keep your eyes peeled, you'll find here and there a word making a repeat appearance. Some words seemed apt or indispensable for use in more than one test or context.

Do the tests become progressively harder?

That is for you to determine. We've placed a number of the more challenging tests toward the back of the book, and we think the

Quizzicles (see page 8) are, in their sequence, increasingly tricky for the most part. Since spellers differ in their strengths and weaknesses, it is difficult to predict how hard (or harder) a test will be for a particular individual. In passing, we'll just mention here that three categorical tests (i.e., those focusing on one type of word, spelling problem, subject area, etc.) in particular, taken together or one after another might bring some people closer to temporary insanity than any of the other tests. (Merely devising, editing, and rechecking their words brought one of us very close to, well, a mental 911 call.)

Moreover, you should feel free to jump around in these pages, taking tests of any kind and in any order that impulse prompts you to.

Dictionary Gargoyles

One way to concoct "hard" spelling tests—it is not our approach—would be to mine the dustier pages of an unabridged dictionary for its more obscure, rarefied words, scarcely ever seen, heard, or imagined to exist. Words so alien in sound or look that one might call them dictionary gargoyles. What constitutes a dictionary gargoyle is definitely debatable, subjective, and all that. In any case, in this book we hope we haven't unwittingly included too many of them. (You should find by far most of the spelling words selected for these pages in at least one of the college dictionaries found everywhere in bookstores.)

In short, a fiendishly unfamiliar and alien-looking word is not at all the same as a fiendishly good spelling test word.

That said, we hope you find the tests challenging enough—and challenging in ever-fresh ways. These tests were not composed for people who memorize the dictionary or who have the time to do that. Are there words you think you can spell but that you become unsure about when you see them next to kindred or "decoy" words that only confuse you? Are you usually right about whether a word's correct ending is *-er* or *-or*? How about those *-os* or *-oes* endings? Or the *-ie* or *-ei* dilemmas? You'll get your chance here to prove your prowess in such matters (and to meet quite a few decoy words, too).

Field Tests

Most spelling tests or quizzes and bees, wherever one encounters them, have a miscellaneous content. But in these pages you'll also come upon a few specialist or topic-focused challenges that address how well you know nomenclature and proper names from the arts and sciences.

If spelling makes you hungry, there is an improbably eclectic mixed-cuisine "menu" for you to correct. You also have a chance here to see how well you spell the vexing names of certain American cities and to test your orthography in world geography.

Quizzicles, Fluster Clusters, and Killer Bees

Quizzicles, Fluster Clusters, Killer Bees—any one of these challenges has the potential to take down a highly confident or big-vocabularied man or woman.

Quizzicles—more than a hundred of them—are a unique feature of this book, and you will not easily escape them. But we hope you won't want to. Quizzicles are mini-tests of only three or five words. They appear throughout, offering repeatedly a kind of impromptu, on-the-fly skirmish to test your—rapid response?—spelling skills. Some of them have one particular word (out of the three or five) that is a bit of a booby trap. Let's just say, most of the Quizzicles are reminders of the many—too many—confusing and exasperatingly different ways English (with all its welcomed foreign borrowings) has to represent in spelling a single sound.

Can you take on a Quizzicle and spell all three or five words correctly? In under, say (respectively), three or five minutes?

Fluster Clusters are short passages—a brief discursive change of pace from the listlike formats of other tests. (For their full effect, be sure to read them aloud, even if only to yourself.) The speller's mission here is to detect the misspellings among these discombobulating sentences densely crammed with rhyming words. The words are so clustered as to seem to be approaching a kind of critical mass. Or is it critical mess?

Killer Bees, each only ten words, will be for most people the hardest of the book's tests—again, you'll be the judge. These are gatherings that include some none-too-common words that are uncomfortably similar, confusingly similar, unhingingly similar. (Some are, in fact, identical in their pronunciations.) But how alike are their correct spellings?

How Correct . . . ?

This is spelling, and its demands are absolute. The letter of the law is the law of the letters, only the exact ones.

The standard protocols of correct spelling ("Close doesn't count") are to be observed. If a term is spelled as two words, a one-word or hyphenated answer is incorrect. If a word has an apostrophe in its spelling, it must be part of the written answer. Accent marks must be indicated on words having such marks.

Only spellings shown in the Answers section will be considered correct. (We have no customer service or complaint department in *So You Think You Can Spell?*)

Scoring the Tests

We suggest any of four options in how you score your spelling performance:

1. Maturely Reflective or Philosophical Assessment
Do you consider strict grading to be degrading?

If you do, this option offers you a kind of private, broad-overview way to judge your performance as a speller—something you consider to be your own business and nobody else's. You're somebody who regards spelling challenges not competitively or vaingloriously but as opportunities for or exercises in self-improvement.

Using this approach, you can "score" yourself—verbally, not mathematically—in terms of how you think you did.

After you've finished a test and before turning to the answer pages, estimate how many words you think you got right. (Write the number down.) Then check the answers. Were you close in predicting how many correct spellings you had? Are you content with how many you got right? Surprised? Disappointed? Horrified? Would you conclude that you're—still?—a pretty good speller?

If you were right on the money about how many words you got right on a given test, give yourself some extra credit (in whatever form you choose). Having a good sense of how correct or incorrect your spellings are in a given challenge is an estimable personal asset.

2. Graded Scoring
If you want nothing less than hard numbers here regarding how you do on a test, we suggest the following:

	Excellent	Good	Fair
50-word test	45 or more correct	40–44	33–39
30-word test	27 or more correct	24–26	20–23
25-word test	23 or more correct	20–22	16–19
20-word test	18 or more correct	16–17	13–15
15-word test	14–15 correct	12–13	10–11
10-word test	9–10 correct	8	6–7
3 words or 5 words	Spell all 3 or 5 words correctly or else.		

If your score is a little too consistently less than "Fair" most of the time—well, do we have to spell it out for you? Here's a suggestion: Sudoku.

Once you've got your own graded test results, you can turn your attention to what's *really* important to you: Guessing what score—lower than yours, you hope?—your friend (or sibling, coworker, classmate, fellow spelling bee activist, etc.) Joe or Jane will get on the test as soon as you can give it to them. This hidden agenda is sometimes referred to as invidious comparison, but few of us are entirely free of this character flaw.

3. Your Own Method
(Feel free!)

4. Zen or Yoga Scoring System
Chill. All answers are equal.
  Namaste!

There you have it. Pencils sharpened (or are you brave enough to use a pen?) and a good, stout eraser at hand? If you're ready to get started, turn to page 31.

Or, if you're not yet feeling quite in top spelling trim and could use some citable, factual, historical confirmation as to how and why English spelling is so unfairly tough, just turn the page.

Answers to back-cover quiz: herculean, passementerie, strychnine, tinnitus, bonhomie, tambourine, quisling, centenary, aeolian, and ziggurat.

Why Is English Spelling So Difficult?

(A Brief History)

Why is the orthography of the English language such a senseless, unpredictable muddle and, for so many of us, a continual problem?

"English spelling is the world's most awesome mess," wrote linguist and author Mario Pei some years ago. "In no other language is it possible to get seven different sounds out of a combination of written letters like *ough* (*dough*, *bought*, *bough*, *rough*, *through*, *thorough*, *hiccough*), or conversely, [to] spell a sound like that ordinarily represented by *sh* in fourteen different ways. . . . In no other language would it be possible to write *phtholognyrrh* for *Turner* by using the *phth* of *phthisic*, the *olo* of *colonel*, the *gn* of *gnat* and the *yrrh* of *myrrh*, or to spell, plausibly, *kaughphy* for *coffee*." English, in short, has too many sounds for its twenty-six-letter Roman alphabet.

While solutions to or simplifications of inherent spelling difficulty in English continue to be elusive, explanations as to how and why our written tongue has come to be so crabbedly irregular are not. We have only to take a brief look at the history of our language.

English, fortunately or not, did not emerge as a wondrously logical and phonetically sane creation from Jupiter's head, much less from the edict of an Oxford-Cambridge academy, a book by Noah Webster, or the mind of a strict American schoolmarm.

English vocabulary, and its modes of spelling, is so rich and varied because over the centuries it has drawn its word stock from numerous other languages. The speech we use today began evolving some fifteen hundred years ago on the island of Britain. In that era it was not mere word borrowing or word stealing that formed the language. It was a series of invasions.

Even before the birth of Christ, the Romans had made a foothold in the British Isles. By about AD 75 they had conquered the Britons (who themselves were descended from two different groups of Celtic invaders that arrived centuries earlier). In the fifth century, the Romans had no sooner withdrawn from Britain than the isles were invaded from the coasts of the North Sea by Teutonic (or Germanic) tribes, the Jutes and, primarily, the Saxons and the Angles. Out of this confluence came what we know as Old English.

Over the next two centuries, the Anglo-Saxons for the most part became converts to Christianity and Britain became a center of learning. The Latin alphabet was introduced, replacing a runic one. Old English evolved into three dialects: Mercian (midlands), Northumbrian (north), and West Saxon and Kentish (south). But the ninth century brought fearsome invasions by Norsemen, who spoke a related language. King Alfred the Great was not able to drive the Norse invaders out, but he did halt the advance of their "Danelaw" at a dividing line between London and Chester. (Today's maps still reflect the differences in place names and spellings on either side of this onetime boundary.)

In the ninth and tenth centuries, the Danish areas of Britain were assimilated and England was unified politically. There were four dialects of Old English in use at the time, until that from Wessex gained preeminence and was adopted by church scribes. For a brief period, Anglo-Saxon spelling became homogeneous and above all phonetic, with vowels denoted in a simple way and without silent consonants.

But invasion struck again, this time in 1066, in the form of what we know as the Norman Conquest. Along with the subjugation of the Anglo-Saxons came a profound upheaval in the English language as it had been. With the occupation of the Norman rulers and clergy came the language of northern France, which the nobility established as the language of all government and of the court. The Normans did not suppress English, but now no official standard could be maintained for its spelling. Fewer books (that is, manuscripts) were written, and those that came forth were generally in French or Latin.

But there was a positive side to these developments. Slowly but surely, the two peoples began mixing, and another "invasion" began: that of French words into English, which had remained quite alive if varied in its dialects in particular regions. Though unstandardized, English had grown less and less inflected in its word endings during those years; that is, the troublesome gender of individual words was no longer observed in practice. French, meanwhile, was never adopted by the general citizenry.

By the fourteenth century, English—now Middle English—had taken its place once and for all as the language of Britain. It was now richly infused with French borrowings and possessed a vocabulary whose spellings were anything but consistent or rational; errors by Norman scribes did not help. As for French itself, by the beginning of the fifteenth century it was considered a foreign language in England.

Middle English had several dialects, but the court settled near London, and with a newly centralized government, the London dialect and spellings became standard, both nationally and internationally. Subsequently, the rich cultural vitality of the Renaissance brought to England not only a burgeoning hunger for learning and classical culture and the spirited coining of new words but also the epoch-making discovery of the printing press.

But printing in no wise encouraged an immediate standardizing of spelling, for several reasons. Consistency of spelling was not considered all that important; the Elizabethan compositors, or typesetters, were given to altering spellings even within the same page or line for space-filling or line-balancing reasons; and many of the early printers in England were from Germany or Holland, were poorly educated, and did not know English well. Moreover, different printers favored different spellings. Shakespeare's works, with all their variant spellings, exemplify the situation at the time. There are thirteen known different spellings of Shakespeare's name recorded, and in the first printing of his sonnets (1609) the word *mistress* was spelled five different ways.

Progress in the standardization of spelling, or at least in awareness of the need for it, was made in the sixteenth and seventeenth centuries because of the publications and proposals of various scholars. But when printing houses finally began to agree on standard spellings, those spellings had often long ceased to reflect the actual pronunciation then prevalent.

Spelling books were printed and became popular. In the early eighteenth century, consideration was given to creating an English Academy (like the French Academy, founded in 1635) to safeguard and regulate language, but most English people did not take kindly to the idea of official meddling with the language, and the idea never got very far.

By the time Samuel Johnson's milestone *A Dictionary of the English*

Language was published in 1755, English spelling was fairly standardized. Although Johnson himself cannot be credited with making spelling uniform, his dictionary was important because it gained wide acceptance and greatly helped to settle or crystallize many spellings. Yet Johnson's primary basis for spellings in his dictionary was etymology, not phonetic aptness, simplicity, or consistency.

Unfortunately, English pronunciation had continued to change rapidly, especially that of its vowels. When an established spelling had finally been achieved, it was often unphonetic, not reflective of actual speech in the land. Also, many words had extraneous or silent letters inserted into them to make them more presentable etymologically— that is, to make their Greek, Latin, or French origin more evident— making spelling yet more unphonetic.

Nonetheless, the dictionary thus became an institution in the eighteenth century, and henceforth the growing middle class sought in it and from it "correctness" in speech and spelling. In addition, English replaced Latin as the language of scholarship, and various "authoritative" grammars were subsequently published that contributed to spelling standardization.

Meanwhile, an ocean away, America was developing its own speechways. Noah Webster's importance to uniform—and often different— spelling in the United States derives not only from his famed *American Dictionary of the English Language* (1828) but also from his *The American Spelling Book* (1783–85). The latter became a veritable bible to Americans, underwent several hundred revisions, and sold more than sixty million copies. At first Webster followed Johnson's (British) spellings—for example, *honour* rather than *honor*. But he included in his dictionary the variant spellings that came to be preferred by Americans, and he ultimately became an influential advocate of American independence in its language and orthography.

In Brief, Ten Reasons Why
English Spelling Is So Confused

1. English is a rich but mongrel language, drawn from other languages having different pronunciation and spelling systems. Alphabetically, it possesses too many sounds (more than forty) for too few letters (twenty-six) in its Roman alphabet.

2. The written word could not keep up with the spoken word. Pronunciation over the centuries underwent many periods of change too rapidly for a truly phonetic spelling to keep abreast. Sometimes, even as a spelling was becoming standardized in print, the word's pronunciation was changing.

3. Authoritative opinions regarding proper spelling have often differed, with some favoring simplified, phonetically appropriate orthography but others maintaining that, above all, spelling should manifest etymology—that is, a word's derivation.

4. At times, letters were inserted into words (by analogy with other words) to make them more etymologically sound, a detraction from actual pronunciation; in many instances the supposed etymology (until modern times a science based very much on guesswork) was erroneous.

5. The Norman Conquest, and French as a new language of court and government, ultimately enriched the language but profoundly disrupted the basis (Old English) for a stabilized spelling in Britain. (To the Norman influence, English owes the letters *j*, *q*, *v*, and *z*; but now *c* was written for *s*, *o* for *u*, and *ou* for *u*, or long *u*.)

6. The advent of printing and proliferation of books brought with them some orthographic stability but also much confusion. Early compositors were often German or Dutch, and different printing houses followed different spelling practices.

7. For many years spelling was arbitrary and thought to be of little importance.

8. The spellings in Samuel Johnson's influential dictionary (1755), which became a world-famous model for lexicographers, were based largely on etymology, not on actual pronunciation.

9. In America, Noah Webster's legendary American dictionary (1828) greatly simplified and standardized U.S. spelling. But to foster better sales of his dictionaries in England, Webster sometimes left less simple British spellings untouched.

10. Proposals over the centuries for the reform of English spelling have never won sustained support. To most people, it seems impracticable to overhaul an entire language and its history. Proposed systems of phonetic spelling seem either too simplistic or too complicated. The most eminent proposers and scholars have found themselves in violent disagreement. And the idea of devising a spelling system based on actual pronunciation always founders on the most problematical of all questions related to orthographic reform: based on whose pronunciation?

Who Was Webster?

Just as we rarely think of spelling without thinking of dictionaries, we rarely think of dictionaries without conjuring up the name *Webster*.

The man behind the name was Noah Webster (1758–1843). The acknowledged father of American lexicography, Webster was (we are apt to forget) a contemporary of George Washington, Thomas Jefferson, Benjamin Franklin, and James Fenimore Cooper.

Webster's life was anything but dry as a reference book. Tendentious and always self-promoting, this contentious patriot was continually a focal point of controversy regarding the American language and its spelling. And his career in many ways epitomizes the many fundamental—and perennially unresolved, it seems—questions and hackles raised when men and women zealously attempt to plan, guide, or protect their national language: Should the language of the United States be thought of as different from that of England, as "the American language"? Should American pronunciation, ideally, be nationally uniform? Should dialects and the borrowing of foreign words be discouraged? Should a dictionary promulgate newly simplified spellings if its citizen readers are already accustomed to more difficult but established spellings?

Webster, a graduate of Yale, was a lawyer and a teacher and wrote not only about language (he had some familiarity with more than twenty languages) but also about economics, religion, medicine (the causes of yellow fever), and politics. His name became well-known with the publication in 1783 of his *The American Spelling Book*, or "blue-backed speller," which had many successive editions and became an enormously popular schoolbook in the United States, second only to the Bible in sales. (Fifty years later, when the U.S. population was less than twenty-five million, it was selling more than a million copies a year.) The book from the PBS television series "The Story of English" gives us a glimpse of Noah Webster at work:

> The success of the American Speller gave Webster, on a royalty of one cent per copy, more than enough to live on, and he now devoted the rest of his life to the zealous championing of the cause of the American language, its spelling, its grammar and its pronunciation. The story is told, by an old printer recalling his apprenticeship, of the day "a little pale-faced man came into the office and handed me a printed slip, saying 'My lad, when you use these words, please oblige me by spelling them as here: theater, center, etc.'" It was Noah Webster traveling about the printing offices and persuading people to follow his "improved" conventions.

Webster published his first dictionary in 1806 and his great two-volume work, *An American Dictionary of the English Language*, in 1828, when he was seventy years old. The latter, however, containing some twelve thousand words not found in any current British dictionary, became a success only in revised editions after Webster's death.

Webster's views regarding the lexicon of our language were strong but shifting ones, and his ideas generated controversy throughout his lifetime. He at first rejected ideas of reforming, or Americanizing, English spelling, favoring such literations as *honour*, *metre*, and *wag-*

gon and expressing respect for Samuel Johnson's illustrious dictionary (1755) as a spelling and pronunciation guide.

But more and more, Webster saw his mission as fostering—through Congress, education, and books—an American language that would be independent and as uniform as possible. He wanted not just to take note of dialects around the country but also to discourage them. He foresaw British and American English diverging into separate languages—all well and good, he felt, as he did not want the standard for American speech to come from London. Ideally, nationally, Webster felt, spelling should not be at odds with pronunciation. It should be reformed (and now was the time to act) through the dissemination of books—his own books. He generally opposed introducing new letters into our alphabet, but at one point recommended adding "eth" (th), "esh" (sh), "eng" (ng), and "ezh" (si or su) and using a small mark to distinguish the voiced th from the unvoiced one. To simplify English spelling, he said, it was necessary to get rid of all silent letters (e.g., to write ment instead of meant); to supplant indefinite letters or letter combinations with definite ones (e.g., greev instead of grieve, korus instead of chorus); and to add certain marks (over or through standard letters) to distinguish between sounds when necessary, as in the case of the voiced or unvoiced th. Unfortunately, some of Webster's proposed new spellings were based on his inspired but erroneous etymologies.

Webster was always pragmatic enough to believe in gradual rather than sudden change in spelling. From the days when he first communicated with Benjamin Franklin, he hoped that Congress would adopt and implement his proposals. It was not to be. As George Philip Krapp notes in The English Language in America, the American public did not welcome such complications, and the aging Franklin did not share Webster's zeal.

Webster's ideas for a so-called Federal English never came to fruition, and in old age he found himself softening his position—not least of all, it has been pointed out, in order not to jeopardize sales of his dictionaries in England. (Among Websterian spellings that were retracted in later editions of his dictionaries were *iz*, *relm*, *mashine*, *yeer*, *bilt*, *tung*, *breth*, *helth*, *beleeve*, and *wimmen*.)

Then, as today, philologists had strong opinions pro or con regarding such "solutions" in matters of language, and Webster's strong Anglophobic views gained him enemies, ridicule, and even parody from many quarters for many years. He was not only an ambitious and, to many, abrasive man but also a self-contradictory one. He repeatedly accused others of stealing his ideas or work. He often purported to have an objective, descriptivist view of American speech, yet continually insisted on perfecting the national tongue. Webster was, H. L. Mencken has noted, "not only a pedagogue but also a Calvinist, and a foe of democracy. Indeed, all his attacks on authority were arguments against the other fellow's and in favor of his own."

In many ways Webster personifies the ambivalence and insecurities many Americans felt for a half century and more after the Revolution regarding superiority or inferiority vis-à-vis England and Europe (notably France, which had a famed language academy but whose tongue Webster described as being enfeebled and not virile in sound). In 1824, while preparing his great two-volume dictionary of 1828, he visited England and made overtures to British scholars in hopes of resolving some differences between the two language camps. He now seemed to stress how similar the two species of English were; there was one English language, not two. His 1829 *Elementary Spelling Book* avowed that its pronunciations generally accorded with those of "well-bred" people in both countries.

The latter part of Webster's career was marked by a heated rivalry between him and lexicographer Joseph Worcester (1784–1865), who had worked for Webster but was a respected scholar in his own right and published his own first dictionary in 1830. Unlike Webster, Worcester was an Anglophile and had a conservative, Johnsonian, and fairly temperate and objective approach to the recording of the language; he preferred more established spellings and more refined pronunciations. (It also happened that Webster and his enterprises were identified with Yale, Worcester and his with Harvard.) Their personal differences—Webster was the aggressor, typically—grew into a celebrated "war of the dictionaries," which continued for two decades after Webster's death in 1843. The war was ultimately very much a commercial one: a no-holds-barred struggle, with unscrupulous tactics, for the American dictionary market. Worcester published his worthy *A Universal and Critical Dictionary of the English Language* in 1846, three years after Webster's death, after which the battle of the books became especially intense. In 1860 Worcester's greatest dictionary appeared, *A Dictionary of the English Language.*

Ultimately, commercial victory went to the Webster line of dictionaries, which had become Merriam-Webster by the turn of the century, but not without irony. (The printers and booksellers George and Charles Merriam secured the rights to Webster's magnum opus in 1843 as well as to any future revised editions.) Much of Noah Webster's own work (including many of his controversial spellings and erroneous etymologies) was done away with, and the more prudent and elegant virtues of Worcester's approach were borrowed by Webster's publishers to achieve success in the marketplace.

For all his autocratic tetchiness, we owe Webster a great deal. He had the vision to realize that American English should and would develop along its own lines. Despite his inclination to "purify" the language in sundry ways, he realized that dictionaries should be guided by actual usage, that new words—Americanisms—are not always needless or "low," and that the pronunciation of place names should be determined by local residents.

Webster also recognized that Americans, more than the British, would look to books—dictionaries—for guidance in matters of language. Many of the spelling revisions he sanctioned (*frolic, physic, center, theater, honor, favor, traveled* and *traveling, check, mask, defense*) have been adopted by Americans, as have certain American pronunciations (*schedule* and *lieutenant*).

Webster, Mencken says in *The American Language,* "was too shrewd to believe that language could really be brought under the yoke. He had observed that it was a living organism with a way of life of its own— with a process of evolution but little determined by purely rational considerations."

Even in Merriam-Webster dictionaries today, the only meaning you will find for the word *webster* is that of weaver, for which *webster* is an archaic term. But for many people the name *Webster* is synonymous with lexicon—or an American one—just as *Baedeker* is with *travel guidebook.*

In the later years of the twentieth century, Merriam-Webster fought to retain exclusive right to the use of the name *Webster* on a dictionary cover but lost in the courts. Today, any lexicon may call itself a Webster's dictionary.

Simplified Spelling, Anyone?

If you continually struggle with spelling, you may now and then have gritted your teeth, bitten the eraser off your pencil, and had a brilliant idea. Instead of your having to improve your spelling, why doesn't somebody improve—simplify—the exasperating orthography of the English language?

Neither Noah Webster nor Benjamin Franklin succeeded in overhauling our alphabet. But that was more than 150 years ago. Why hasn't there been a law passed to rid English of all useless silent letters, unnecessary double l's and double t's, and that -able or -ible mess?

Why not indeed.

Reforming our way of spelling would, it has been argued, save time and expense in elementary education and in all writing and printing. It would allow people to spell as they pronounce, and possibly focus more attention on good pronunciation and make it more standardized everywhere. It would make it easier for foreigners to become Americanized (or Anglicized) and make English a more accessible international language. Words now spelled the same but having different meanings, such as *bow*, *tear*, *lead*, and *sow*, would be differentiated (although there would be an impractical, troublesome vice versa, namely, a blurring of distinctions between, say, *to*, *two*, and *too*).

A simple and sanely phonetic English spelling system would save both pupils and teachers a lot of grief. It might even, one proponent has vowed, spare children the "atrophy of logical faculties"—so illogical is the morass of our present spelling.

The history of our language shows that not only born misspellers but exasperated English and English-as-a-second-language teachers and professors, foreign students, and copyeditors have had the same original thought. Spelling reform has been passionately espoused, opposed, and debated over the past two hundred years, involving not only Benjamin Franklin and Webster but Sir Isaac Pitman; Mark Twain; George Bernard Shaw; Alfred, Lord Tennyson; and Teddy Roosevelt. But it has remained an *ignis fatuus*, a perennially lost cause.

Proposals to homogenize our orthography go back to the beginning of the thirteenth century (before printing was introduced into England, in 1476, by William Caxton). A monk named Ormin, or Orm, ventured some simplified spellings in his *Ormulum*, a work in Middle English paraphrasing the Scriptures. Orm's intent was to make the written word reflect pronunciation more accurately. He doubled consonants after short vowels, retaining single consonants after long vowels. Thus he spelled *fire fir* and *fir firr*. Orm spelled the Middle English word for "went," pronounced with a long *o*, *for*, whereas the preposition we know as *for* he spelled *forr*. But—possibly a harbinger of reactions to later high-minded reform efforts—Orm's ideas did not catch on.

In the sixteenth century, Sir John Cheke, a professor of Greek at Cambridge University, urged ridding the language of silent final *e*'s and all silent consonants (e.g., *dout* instead of *doubt*). But despite his having influential support, English, as H. L. Mencken later put it in *The American Language*, "went on its wild way." In the following century, John Wilkins's "Essay Towards a Real Character and a Philosophical Language" (1668) proposed a new, international phonetic alphabet without success. (Wilkins was a Cambridge master and later a bishop.) And exactly a hundred years later, encouraged by Webster, Franklin devised his alphabet but never published the document, confessing that he felt too old for such a crusade. As for Webster, his views changed over the years. Initially opposing any spelling changes, he favored considerable reform by 1790, then came to advocate only moderate (and inconsistent) changes.

Since then, in both England and the United States, many others have put forth spelling reform schemes. They have ranged from systems of radically new phonetic symbols (some like those of shorthand) to less ambitious modifications of the alphabet or of particular common words.

Among the numerous post-Revolution and Victorian American individuals hopeful of respelling our language were (to name a few of them) Jonathan Fisher, a clergyman and artist; William Thornton, a Scottish physician in the United States; James Ewing, a businessman; Abner Kneeland, a Baptist minister and later a freethinker; Michael H. Barton, a Quaker educator; Ezekiel Rich, a minister; and Amasa D. Sproat, a druggist.

In the twentieth century, reform was promoted by various organizations on both sides of the Atlantic, most notably by the Simplified Spelling Board in the United States and the Simplified Spelling Society, based in England—all to no end.

We may also mention Anglic, a Swedish project to adapt, or "generalize," English for worldwide use. Though the project was endorsed in London in 1930 by the International Phonetic Association and other groups, it was not a phonetic system, and the rival Simplified Spelling Board was not so enthusiastic about it. With the death of its deviser, R. E. Zachrisson, and the advent of World War II, its promotion came to a halt.

Spelling reform, however well intentioned or ingenious the plan, has found support neither with the British nor with the American citizenry. More often than not, its advocates have quarreled over methods or specifics, and more often than not, the great misspelling populace has remained mightily indifferent, resistant, or bemused regarding such meddling with our time-honored language. Another curious fact is that most reformist ideologues have not practiced—or spelled—what they preached in their own writings and correspondence.

Why, finally, do most people oppose or even ridicule the idea of changing our approved spellings? It seems to come down to the truth, sad or not, that such an undertaking, here and now in the twenty-first century, is too quixotic—either too little too late or too much too late; and to the fact that to many people, the most idealistic and educated spelling reformer is some sort of crank.

Rest assured, nonetheless, the spelling reform movement will never be stone dead. (Even in our new millennium, die-hard advocates of simplified spelling continue to show up as picketers at the finals of the Scripps National Spelling Bee in Washington, DC, to protest—what else?—spelling bees.)

If it has made no other lasting dent in our language, the spelling reform movement has probably in some way encouraged the endemic whimsical, quasi-phonetic, or truncated spellings, such as *lite*, that we see everywhere in branding and advertising and, above all, in the shorthand of informal Internet and cell phone communication today. (Broken English of a different and simpler sort used to be called *telegraphese*.) Is this computer-age lingua franca not only unquestionably indispensable but also creative and imaginative? Is it linguistically fascinating or is it brashly impatient and lazy English?

Will this—radically—"simplified" form of techno-English eventually aid the cause of a more considered, canonic spelling reform? Or is it fated not only to prove how fatuous the notion of simplified spelling is but also to be immeasurably erosive to orthodox English spelling itself?

The Tests

❀ Spelling Warm-Up 1

Circle the correct spelling.

1. a. gumption   b. gummtion   11. a. gizzard   b. gizzerd
2. a. gallivant   b. galivant   12. a. scintilating   b. scintillating
3. a. mischievious   b. mischievous   13. a. absorbtion   b. absorption
4. a. introvert   b. intravert   14. a. exhileration   b. exhilaration
5. a. hommage   b. homage   15. a. appraisle   b. appraisal
6. a. aching   b. acheing   16. a. vacuum   b. vaccuum
7. a. vassal   b. vassall   17. a. superintendant   b. superintendent
8. a. larangitis   b. laryngitis   18. a. separate   b. seperate
9. a. excerpt   b. exerpt   19. a. tarrif   b. tariff
10. a. pittence   b. pittance   20. a. priviledge   b. privilege

❀ Spelling Warm-Up 2

Circle the correct spelling.

1. a. heterageniety   b. hetrogeniety   c. heterogeneity
2. a. ansillary   b. ancelary   c. ancillary
3. a. casuistry   b. cassuistry   c. casouistry
4. a. mallese   b. mallaise   c. malaise
5. a. undiscried   b. undescried   c. undiscride
6. a. beatific   b. beyatific   c. beautific
7. a. sateyity   b. satteity   c. satiety
8. a. shicanery   b. chicanery   c. chickanery
9. a. frangeable   b. frangable   c. frangible

10. **a.** taigga   **b.** teiga   **c.** taiga

11. **a.** cutanious   **b.** cutaneous   **c.** queutaneous

12. **a.** desuetude   **b.** dessuitude   **c.** dessuetude

13. **a.** millipede   **b.** milopede   **c.** millepede

14. **a.** paucity   **b.** pauscity   **c.** pausety

15. **a.** bucolic   **b.** buccolic   **c.** bucollic

16. **a.** capillary   **b.** cappillary   **c.** cappilary

17. **a.** ubiquitous   **b.** eubiquitous   **c.** ubiquetous

18. **a.** apogee   **b.** apoge   **c.** appogie

19. **a.** sizemometer   **b.** sysmometer   **c.** seismometer

20. **a.** onerous   **b.** onorous   **c.** onnorous

❇ Spelling Warm-Up 3

Circle the correct spelling.

1. **a.** antihistamine   **b.** antehystamine   **c.** antihistomine   **d.** antihystamine

2. **a.** heifer   **b.** heffor   **c.** heffer   **d.** heiffer

3. **a.** agglomeration   **b.** aglomoration   **c.** agglommeration   **d.** aglommeration

4. **a.** paniscea   **b.** pannasea   **c.** panacea   **d.** panascea

5. **a.** catyclism   **b.** caticlism   **c.** cataclysm   **d.** cateclysm

6. **a.** talasman   **b.** talisman   **c.** tallesman   **d.** talesmine

7. **a.** vellum   **b.** velume   **c.** vellom   **d.** velum

8. **a.** appothicary   **b.** apothecary   **c.** appothecary   **d.** apothacary

9. **a.** affadavet   **b.** affidavit   **c.** afidavitt   **d.** afidavet

10. **a.** toccsin   **b.** tocksin   **c.** tocsin   **d.** toksin

11. **a.** codicil   **b.** codisil   **c.** codicile   **d.** codecill

12. **a.** aborration   **b.** aberration   **c.** aberation   **d.** abberration

13. **a.** synosure	**b.** seinosur	**c.** cynosure	**d.** signosure
14. **a.** dennazen	**b.** denizen	**c.** dennizen	**d.** denezen
15. **a.** lagniappe	**b.** laniape	**c.** lanaippe	**d.** lanniap
16. **a.** apiery	**b.** apiary	**c.** appiari	**d.** apierry
17. **a.** fasicule	**b.** fassicle	**c.** fascicule	**d.** fascicle
18. **a.** viand	**b.** viande	**c.** vyande	**d.** vyonde
19. **a.** aquiescent	**b.** acquiescent	**c.** aquiesant	**d.** aquiescent
20. **a.** mallidiction	**b.** malediction	**c.** malodiction	**d.** maladiction

❃ Three-Word Quizzicles 1–5

The words in each of these wee bees have not been idly chosen.
Write in the correct spelling.

One

1. kar-ee-O-kuh   _____

   (variation of the samba)

2. KAR-uh-kole   _____

   (half-turn maneuver by a mounted horse)

3. kar-ee-O-kee   _____

   (entertainment for amateur singers using a musical accompaniment device)

> *Someone asked a Fool: "Is kebab with a or o?"*
> *"With meat," he answered.*
>
> —Anonymous (Sufi humor)

Two

1. TOO-too   _____
   (short skirt of a ballerina)

2. FROO-froo   _____
   (frills or finery)

3. MOO-moo   _____
   (loose and brightly colored or patterned dress originated in Hawaii)

Three

1. uh-PLUM   _____
   (easy self-assurance or poise)

2. KAHR-duh-mum   _____
   (aromatic condiment from Asia)

3. MAH-dik-um   _____
   (small or minimal amount)

Four

1. SLUJ-ee   _____
   (of or like sludge)

2. JOW-lee   _____
   (having jowls)

3. CHAN-see   _____
   (uncertain or risky)

Five

1. **TRUN-chun** _____

   (police officer's club or billy)

2. **PIJ-un** _____

   (simplified blend of two languages, based mostly on one of them)

3. **KAY-jun** _____

   (pertaining to Louisianans descended from French-speaking emigrants from Canada)

❊ Multiple Choice 1

Circle the correct spelling.

1. **a.** delliquess   **b.** deliquese   **c.** delliquesce   **d.** deliquesce

   (to dissolve or melt)

2. **a.** hoi polloi   **b.** hoy palloi   **c.** hoy polloi   **d.** hoi palloi

   (the common crowd, the masses)

3. **a.** dipphthongal   **b.** dipfthongal   **c.** dipthongal   **d.** diphthongal

   (pertaining to a gliding of vowels)

4. **a.** parasole   **b.** parosole   **c.** parasall   **d.** parasol

   (woman's light umbrella or sunshade)

5. **a.** litterateur   **b.** litterator   **c.** literateur   **d.** literatteur

   (literary person or seasoned writer)

6. **a.** lachet   **b.** latchet   **c.** latchette   **d.** lachette

   (fastening strap on a shoe)

7. **a.** cerrulian   **b.** cerulian   **c.** cerullian   **d.** cerulean

    (sky blue)

8. **a.** palymcest   **b.** palempsest   **c.** palimpsest   **d.** palymcest

    (papyrus, parchment, etc., on which earlier writing can be detected)

9. **a.** crackelure   **b.** craquellour   **c.** craquillure   **d.** craquelure

    (surface cracks on a painting)

10. **a.** reohstat   **b.** rheostat   **c.** rheostatt   **d.** reohstatt

    (electric current regulator)

11. **a.** farinah   **b.** farrinah   **c.** farrina   **d.** farina

    (meal used as breakfast cereal)

12. **a.** paparazi   **b.** papparrazi   **c.** paparazzi   **d.** papparazzi

    (celebrity-pursuing photographers)

13. **a.** parreur   **b.** parure   **c.** pareur   **d.** parrure

    (matching set of jewels, ornaments, etc.)

14. **a.** inchoat   **b.** inchoate   **c.** incoate   **d.** incoite

    (not completely formed or manifested)

15. **a.** cunaeiform   **b.** cuneiform   **c.** cuneaform   **d.** cunnaeiform

    (using wedge-shaped characters for an alphabet)

16. **a.** murmidon   **b.** murrmidon   **c.** myrmidon   **d.** myrrmidon

    (obedient or unquestioning subordinate)

17. **a.** kaleidoscopic   **b.** kelaidoscopic   **c.** kalleidoscopic   **d.** kaleidascopic

    (showing changing colors or patterns)

18. **a.** megilah   **b.** meggilah   **c.** megillah   **d.** megilla

    (long and involved story)

19. **a.** mah-jong   **b.** majong   **c.** ma-jonng   **d.** mah-jongg

    (game of Chinese origin using 144 tiles)

20. **a.** bêttise   **b.** bêtise   **c.** baetise   **d.** bêttize

    (stupid act)

❀ Word and Definition Match 1

Match each (numbered) word on the left with its correct (lettered) definition on the right. Each numbered word has, also in the left column, a soundalike but differently spelled "mate"—with a different meaning.

1. spoor	**a.** writing paper	_____		
2. augur	**b.** not moving	_____		
3. rillettes	**c.** reproductive body	_____		
4. principle	**d.** style	_____		
5. forward	**e.** main or chief	_____		
6. tort	**f.** rich dessert cake	_____		
7. minor	**g.** seasoned ground-meat appetizer	_____		
8. stationery	**h.** nonadult	_____		
9. flair	**i.** fundamental assumption or tenet	_____		

10. flare	j. streamlets	_____
11. stationary	k. ahead	_____
12. miner	l. in law, a wrongful act	_____
13. complement	m. prefatory part of a book	_____
14. spore	n. tool for boring	_____
15. rillets	o. foretell	_____
16. torte	p. flattering remark	_____
17. auger	q. coal worker	_____
18. principal	r. animal trace or droppings	_____
19. foreword	s. something that completes	_____
20. compliment	t. illuminating blaze	_____

> The Roman alphabet has always been inadequate for the phonetic representation of the English language, most strikingly so for Modern English. We have, for example, only five vowel symbols, a, e, i, o, and u; that this number is wholly inadequate is indicated by the fact that the first of these alone may have as many as six different sound values, as in cat, came, calm, any, call, and was (riming with fuzz).
>
> —Thomas Pyles and John Algeo

❊ Five-Word Quizzicles 1–3

The words in each of these wee bees have not been idly chosen.
Write in the correct spelling.

One

1. **AK-wuh-dukt**   _____

   (*structure conveying flowing water*)

2. **AK-wuf-er**   _____

   (*subterranean mineral stratum having water*)

3. **AK-wuh-veet**   _____

   (*clear liquor of Scandinavia*)

4. **AK-wuh-lyn**   _____

   (*eaglelike or curved like an eagle's beak*)

5. **AK-wee-us**   _____

   (*pertaining to water*)

> . . . the Marquess of Queensberry made his way to the Albemarle Club, where he left his card, endorsed "To Oscar Wilde posing as a somdomite"—a misspelling which was to become famous. The porter, with wise discretion, put the card in an envelope, and ten days later handed it to Wilde when he visited the club. As he handed it over, he calmly assured the recipient that he had not understood what it meant.
>
> —Martin Fido

Two

1. kor-EEN   _____

   (chorus girl)

2. buh-GEEN   _____

   (ballroom dance similar to the rumba)

3. vuh-TREEN   _____

   (partly glass cabinet or showcase for objects)

4. DA-muh-seen   _____

   (pertaining to damask)

5. ter-EEN   _____

   (earthly)

Three

1. gon-duh-LEER   _____

   (one who propels a gondola)

2. sah-nuh-TEER   _____

   (composer of sonnets)

3. pis-tuh-LEER   _____

   (one bearing or using a pistol)

4. lah-vuh-LEER   _____

   (pendant worn on a neck chain)

5. BEL-vuh-deer   _____

   (structure or site having a pleasing view)

❃ Say It and Spell It 1

Write in the correct spelling.

1. **MAR-dee-grah** _____
   (pre-Lent carnival period)

2. **OUT-ly-er** _____
   (one living elsewhere from where his or her business is)

3. **SAF-fy-er** _____
   (usually but not necessarily blue gem)

4. **WIL-fuh-lee** _____
   (perversely or obstinately)

5. **WIL-ful-ness** _____
   (perverseness or obstinacy)

6. **ER-uh-gwy** _____
   (South American country)

7. **trans-MIS-uh-bul** _____
   (passable, as a disease)

8. **zhuh-LAY** _____
   (cosmetic gel)

9. **TREE-klee** _____
   (cloyingly sweet)

10. **TERT-lit** _____
    (small turtle)

11. FOR-mat-er   _____

    (one who devises a format)

12. uh-BIZ-mul   _____

    (profoundly low, deep, or bad)

13. per-spik-AY-shus   _____

    (keenly perceptive)

14. uh-NEEL   _____

    (to strengthen through heating and cooling)

15. PAR-uf   _____

    (flourish at the end of a signature)

16. BRAYZD   _____

    (cooked slowly in fat in a closed pot)

17. muh-KAD-um   _____

    (type of road surface containing broken stone)

18. dis-KUM-fit-er   _____

    (one who disturbs or frustrates)

19. KAR-ul   _____

    (study cubicle)

20. AN-uh-dyn   _____

    (relieving pain or soothing)

❀ Fluster Cluster 1

Circle the misspelled words.

In Paris, the pianist at the Swan Club, with its historic oubliette near the celleret and mono-grammed tabaret bankettes (florets around a coronet-crowned cygnet), played a jazzy minuet bal musette style while a lonely grisette with castanets and unsteady soubrette (from Latvia, a Lette) did slow pirouettes—not exactly au faite. In a red blazer with epaulets and a yellow aiguillette and sporting a lorgnette, he sipped at his annisette, winding up his set before the nonnet (with two cornets) made their entrance in dramatic silhouette.

❀ Three-Word Quizzicles 6–10

The words in each of these wee bees have not been idly chosen.
   Write in the correct spelling.

Six

1. ruh-KO-ko   _____
   (pertaining to the elaborated curved and ornamental eighteenth-century Western architectural style)

2. PIK-uh-lo   _____
   (small flute with a higher range than the conventional flute)

3. pek-uh-DIL-o   _____
   (minor sin or misdeed)

Seven

1. muh-THOO-suh-luh _____

   (Noah's long-living ancestor)

2. shuh-her-uh-ZAHD _____

   (fictional sultan's wife who relates the Arabian Nights *tales)*

3. ag-uh-MEM-non _____

   (in mythology, Greek leader at Troy)

Eight

1. tuh-MAH-lee _____

   (steamed wrap of cornmeal with ground beef or beans)

2. tim-BAH-lees _____

   (pair of Afro-Cuban drums played with drumsticks)

3. tuh-MAH-lee _____

   (liver of the lobster)

Nine

1. BAHK-uh-nal _____

   (drunken revelry or orgy)

2. bar-uh-KOO-duh _____

   (elongated predatory marine fish)

3. BAK-uh-rah _____

   (casino card game in which players bet against the banker)

Ten

1. LIN-ee-uh-ment   _____

   (physical contour feature, as of a face)

2. LIN-uh-ment   _____

   (preparation used as a skin salve)

3. Lin-EE-un   _____

   (pertaining to the binomial system of scientific nomenclature)

❋ Two Words or One 1

In English, many two-word expressions eventually acquire a hyphen and ultimately become a single unhyphenated word. (The look of a word is a factor here: red ink is not likely to become redink.) It's a constant but unpredictable evolution, if one not true of all compound nouns.

Are the substantives below (per present-day dictionaries) written as two words or as one—currently? You'll doubtless find some of the answers are a bit surprising.

Circle the correct words or word.

1.	snow ball	snowball	7.	film maker	filmmaker
2.	tail light	taillight	8.	pot holder	potholder
3.	back seat	backseat	9.	bird bath	birdbath
4.	red brick	redbrick	10.	hair shirt	hairshirt
5.	waste water	wastewater	11.	locker room	lockerroom
6.	sales clerk	salesclerk	12.	toll booth	tollbooth

13.	step ladder	stepladder	20.	peep hole	peephole
14.	night club	nightclub	21.	art work	artwork
15.	bow tie	bowtie	22.	paper clip	paperclip
16.	bar bell	barbell	23.	pocket knife	pocketknife
17.	hammer lock	hammerlock	24.	sea bird	seabird
18.	law suit	lawsuit	25.	lamp post	lamppost
19.	window sill	windowsill			

❊ Multiple Choice 2

Circle the correct spelling.

1. **a.** sinsimilla   **b.** sinsemilla   c. sensimilla   d. sensemilla
   (type of marijuana)

2. **a.** amersing   **b.** ammercing   c. amercing   d. ammersing
   (punishing by fining)

3. **a.** formaldahyde   **b.** formaldihide   c. formaldehyde   d. formaldihyde
   (gas used in aqueous form as a preservative)

4. **a.** pizzacatto   **b.** pizacatto   c. pizzicato   d. pizzicatto
   (in music, played by plucking the strings)

5. **a.** basinet   **b.** bassinet   c. bassinette   d. basinette
   (basketlike bed for an infant)

6. **a.** farrinacious   **b.** farinaceous   c. farinacious   d. farrinaceous
   (starchy)

7. **a.** hobbeldihoy   **b.** hobbledihoy   c. hobbledehoy   d. hobbledeyhoy
   (awkward or gawky adolescent)

8. **a.** cicaida   **b.** cicada   **c.** ciccaida   **d.** ciccada
(insect that makes a shrill sound)

9. **a.** temerrarious   **b.** temerareous   **c.** temerarious   **d.** temmerarious
(daringly bold)

10. **a.** amethist   **b.** amythist   **c.** amethyst   **d.** amathyst
(violet or purple gemstone)

11. **a.** Pocahontas   **b.** Pocohontas   **c.** Pocohontos   **d.** Poccahontas
(Indian maiden who saved the life of Captain John Smith)

12. **a.** mellinoma   **b.** mellanoma   **c.** melinoma   **d.** melanoma
(molelike malignancy)

13. **a.** cacophany   **b.** cacaphony   **c.** caccophony   **d.** cacophony
(harsh or unpleasant sound)

14. **a.** filiment   **b.** filliment   **c.** fillament   **d.** filament
(electric current conductor or cathode)

15. **a.** somter   **b.** sumpter   **c.** sommter   **d.** sumter
(pack mule, horse, etc.)

16. **a.** tamboureen   **b.** tamboreen   **c.** tamborine   **d.** tambourine
(handheld and shaken percussion instrument)

17. **a.** prosalyte   **b.** prosilyte   **c.** proselyte   **d.** proscilite
(one converted)

18. **a.** bourgoise   **b.** bourgoisée   **c.** bourgeoise   **d.** borgeoise
(female middle-class person)

19. **a.** brasard   **b.** brissarde   c. brassard   d. brassarde
    (armband)

20. **a.** ptetsie fly   **b.** ptetze fly   c. tsetsie fly   d. tsetse fly
    (African fly causing sleeping sickness)

❋ Doubled Letter or No

Circle the correct spelling.

1.	misspelling	mispelling	14.	threshhold	threshold
2.	pasttime	pastime	15.	bookkeeper	bookeeper
3.	nighttime	nightime	16.	roommate	roomate
4.	poettaster	poetaster	17.	headdress	headress
5.	drunkenness	drunkeness	18.	musketteer	musketeer
6.	coattail	coatail	19.	teammate	teamate
7.	morass	morrass	20.	suddenness	suddeness
8.	occurrence	occurence	21.	accommodate	acommodate
9.	withhold	withold	22.	commemmorate	commemorate
10.	dumbbell	dumbell	23.	neccessity	necessity
11.	newsstand	newstand	24.	pusillanimous	pusilanimous
12.	durress	duress	25.	committment	commitment
13.	misshapen	mishapen			

❋ Three-Word Quizzicles 11–15

The words in each of these wee bees have not been idly chosen.
Write in the correct spelling.

Eleven

1. heh-JEM-uh-nee _____
   (reigning or dominantly influential power)

2. uh-NEM-uh-nee _____
   (colorful marine polyp with flowerlike tentacles)

3. HAHM-uh-nee _____
   (soaked hulled kernels of corn)

Twelve

1. WAYN-ryt _____
   (maker of wagons)

2. AK-uh-lyt _____
   (designated assistant to clergy in a religious service)

3. BLATH-er-skyt _____
   (incessantly foolish talker or gabber)

Upon the introduction of printing, indeed, English orthography entered into that realm of Chaos and old Night in which it has ever since been floundering; it then began to put on the shape it at present bears, "if shape it may be called that shape has none."

—Thomas R. Lounsbury

Thirteen

1. lil-uh-PYOO-shun

   (small or miniature)

   _____

2. pik-ee-OON

   (trivial or piddling)

   _____

3. PIG-me-un

   (of or like a small or dwarfish person)

   _____

Fourteen

1. kuh-LAH-sus

   (gigantic statue or any immense thing)

   _____

2. brob-ding-NAY-gee-un

   (huge)

   _____

3. GOO-gul

   (the number 1 followed by 100 zeros)

   _____

Fifteen

1. KAN-uh-kin

   (small can or cup for drinking)

   _____

2. BAWL-duh-kin

   (canopy placed or carried over a venerated person or object)

   _____

3. PEM-uh-kin

   (dried meat as a concentrated food)

   _____

✱ Say It and Spell It 2

Write in the correct spelling.

1. **DIS-tul**   _____
   (anatomically far from the point of attachment)

2. **uh-man-yoo-EN-sees**   _____
   (copyists or dictation takers)

3. **BAY-duh-ker**   _____
   (travel guidebook)

4. **GLAYR-ee**   _____
   (brightly reflective or dazzling)

5. **dy-AL-uh-sis**   _____
   (use of membranes to separate elements of a liquid)

6. **tuh-BAHG-un**   _____
   (sled curved upward at one end)

7. **puh-TROON**   _____
   (old New York or New Jersey estate proprietor)

8. **KAY-tiff**   _____
   (coward)

9. **PRES-shunt**   _____
   (having foresight)

10. **TET-nus**   _____
    (infectious spasmodic disease often affecting jaw muscles)

11. **kuh-may-dee-uh-del-AHR-tee**   _____

    (old Italian comedy genre with stock masked characters and plots)

12. **IM-prest**   _____

    (loan or advance)

13. **PEE-nok-ul**   _____

    (game using a pack of 48 cards)

14. **ahk-sid-i-ZAY-shun**   _____

    (dehydrogenation affected by oxygen)

15. **NUN-kyu-pay-tiv**   _____

    (in law, oral rather than in writing)

16. **DUN**   _____

    (to demand payment)

17. **TWY-nee**   _____

    (like strong string or cord)

18. **KIB-it-zer**   _____

    (unwanted commenter or adviser)

19. **PRAHS-uh-lit-tyz**   _____

    (to convert or recruit)

20. **kuh-KOON**   _____

    (insect's protective envelope)

❊ Five-Word Quizzicles 4–6

The words in each of these wee bees have not been idly chosen.
Write in the correct spelling.

Four

1. WIL-ee-waw _____
   (strong, violent wind or squall)

2. FOO-fuh-raw _____
   (fuss, or friction over something trivial or silly)

3. GYOO-gaw _____
   (showy ornament or trinket)

4. TRAWF _____
   (long V-shaped feed or water receptacle for animals)

5. KOW-tow _____
   (to be deferential or obsequious)

Christine: Dismiss me, madam?
Gardner: Cora, can you be so cruel?
Mrs. Prout: Alas, yes! She has sinned the secretarial sin which is beyond forgiveness.
She has misspelt!
Gardner: Impossible!

—Arnold Bennett, The Stepmother

Five

1. sol-STISH-ul _____

   (pertaining to the beginnings of summer and winter in either hemisphere)

2. in-ter-SPAY-shul _____

   (pertaining to an intervening space or period of time)

3. sur-FISH-ul _____

   (pertaining to a surface or surfaces)

4. kar-uh-PAY-shul _____

   (pertaining to a protective shell or covering of an animal, e.g., a turtle)

5. SEN-uh-shul _____

   (chief steward in a noble household of the Middle Ages)

Six

1. FRIP-uh-ree _____

   (trivial or showy finery)

2. ban-muh-REE _____

   (cooking vessel to hold boiling water and smaller pots)

3. po-puh-REE _____

   (selective mixture, as of aromatic flower petals, spices, etc.)

4. KOHN-juh-reez _____

   (collection or aggregation)

5. kuh-RAHB-uh-ree _____

   (festival of Australia's Aborigines)

✺ Two Spellings Allowed

Three spellings are shown for each of the words defined below. Which two are acceptable?

1. **a.** anurism   **b.** aneurism   **c.** aneurysm
   (abnormal dilatation of a blood vessel)

2. **a.** bourne   **b.** borne   **c.** bourn
   (boundary, goal, or limit)

3. **a.** caravansery   **b.** caravansary   **c.** caravanserai
   (large inn or hostelry)

4. **a.** tumbrill   **b.** tumbril   **c.** tumbrel
   (French Revolution cart bringing condemned prisoners to execution)

5. **a.** weisenheimer   **b.** wisenheimer   **c.** wisinheimer
   (smart aleck)

6. **a.** sillabub   **b.** sillibub   **c.** syllabub
   (sweetened cream-based wine or cider drink)

7. **a.** Manichean   **b.** Manichaean   **c.** Manichian
   (dualistic philosophically regarding good and evil)

8. **a.** absinth   **b.** absanthe   **c.** absinthe
   (strong, toxic green aromatic liqueur)

9. **a.** barcarolle   **b.** barkarolle   **c.** barcarole
   (Venetian gondolier's boat song)

10. **a.** jannisary   **b.** janizary   **c.** janissary
    (elite or unswervingly loyal soldier or follower)

11. **a.** teetotaller   **b.** teatotaller   **c.** teetotaler
(abstainer from alcohol)

12. **a.** cockamamy   **b.** cockamamie   **c.** kockamamy
(senseless or crazy)

13. **a.** kaput   **b.** kapput   **c.** kaputt
(broken, out of action, or not usable)

14. **a.** monniker   **b.** monicker   **c.** moniker
(personal name or nickname)

15. **a.** whodonnit   **b.** whodunnit   **c.** whodunit
(mystery or detective crime novel)

16. **a.** tarbushe   **b.** tarbush   **c.** tarboosh
(usually tasseled red felt Turkish hat similar to the fez)

17. **a.** apennage   **b.** apanage   **c.** appanage
(customary and rightful property, or a perquisite or endowment)

18. **a.** topey   **b.** topee   **c.** topi
(light helmutlike sun hat of pith)

19. **a.** veranda   **b.** verandah   **c.** verannda
(usually extensive and roofed porch along the outside of a building)

20. **a.** sirupy   **b.** syrupy   **c.** syrupey
(cloying in sweetness or sentiment)

❀ Multiple Choice 3

Circle the correct spelling.

1. **a.** flytyer   **b.** flytier   **c.** fly tier   **d.** fly tyer
   (maker of fishing flies)

2. **a.** ensorcellment   **b.** insorsellment   **c.** ensorclement   **d.** insorclement
   (bewitchment)

3. **a.** carrefour   **b.** cariforre   **c.** carrifore   **d.** carefour
   (crossroads or square)

4. **a.** jalapeño   **b.** jaliapeño   **c.** jalliapeño   **d.** jalapenno
   (Mexican pepper)

5. **a.** Roorshach   **b.** Roorschach   **c.** Rorschach   **d.** Rorshach
   (psychological inkblot test)

6. **a.** strycknine   **b.** strichnine   **c.** strychnine   **d.** strichnyne
   (type of poison)

7. **a.** bimilinnary   **b.** bimillinary   **c.** bimilinary   **d.** bimillenary
   (two-thousandth anniversary)

8. **a.** Chehjuajua   **b.** Chihuaua   **c.** Chihuahua   **d.** Chijuahua
   (Mexican breed of small dog with pointed ears)

9. **a.** chatteleine   **b.** chatellaine   **c.** chatelleine   **d.** chatelaine
   (mistress of a large estate or household)

10. **a.** cocotte   **b.** coccotte   **c.** cocqotte   **d.** cocquot
    (prostitute)

11. **a.** schedaddle   **b.** skiddadle   **c.** skidaddle   **d.** skedaddle
   (to run away)

12. **a.** bizarrerie   **b.** bazaarery   **c.** bazaarerie   **d.** bizarrery
   (peculiar happenings, appearance, etc.; strangeness)

13. **a.** nayade   **b.** niade   **c.** naiad   **d.** nyad
   (water sprite)

14. **a.** tai quon do   **b.** tae quon do   **c.** tae kwon do   **d.** tai kwon do
   (Korean martial art)

15. **a.** aolian   **b.** aolean   **c.** aeolian   **d.** aolaean
   (musically making a sighing, windlike sound)

16. **a.** piquaresque   **b.** picaresque   **c.** piccaresque   **d.** picarresque
   (pertaining to the fictional adventures of rogues or rascals)

17. **a.** banquette   **b.** bankette   **c.** bancquette   **d.** banquett
   (upholstered seat built into a wall)

18. **a.** koine   **b.** quoiné   **c.** coiné   **d.** coinei
   (dialect that has spread)

19. **a.** anopheles   **b.** anofeles   **c.** annopheles   **d.** anophelies
   (malaria-causing mosquito)

20. **a.** Asculapian   **b.** Esculapian   **c.** Aeschulapian   **d.** Aesculapian
   (pertaining to the Roman god of medicine or healing)

❊ Three-Word Quizzicles 16–20

The words in each of these wee bees have not been idly chosen.
Write in the correct spelling.

Sixteen

1. RIB-uld   _____

   (coarsely sexual in language)

2. KO-bald   _____

   (in German folklore, an underground-dwelling goblin)

3. KAT-er-wawld   _____

   (wailed or screeched)

Seventeen

1. kuh-RAF   _____

   (flared-lip bottle for holding wine to be served)

2. SEN-uh-taf   _____

   (memorial honoring a person buried)

3. SHAN-dee-gaf   _____

   (a drink, beer mixed with ginger beer or lemonade)

The spelling of words is subordinate. Morbidness for nice spelling and tenac-
ity for or against some one letter or so means dandyism and impotence in
literature.

—Walt Whitman

Eighteen

1. jee-AHD-es-ee   _____

   (mathematics branch dealing with the dimensions and shape of the earth)

2. thee-AHD-es-ee   _____

   (defense of God's goodness despite the existence of evil)

3. PLOOR-uh-see   _____

   (membrane inflammation on the surface of the lung)

Nineteen

1. ba-luh-LY-kuh   _____

   (Russian triangular-bodied, guitarlike instrument)

2. vy-uh-lun-CHEL-o   _____

   (cello)

3. dij-uh-ree-DOO   _____

   (polelike wind instrument of Australia's aborigenes)

Twenty

1. kos-MOG-uh-nee   _____

   (a theory of the universe's origins)

2. pol-LIJ-uh-nee   _____

   (having more than one female mate at the same time)

3. on-TOJ-uh-nee   _____

   (evolutionary development of an individual organism)

❊ To Bee—Or Not to B

When referred to in text, the 21 consonants in our alphabet can be written as the individual letters that they are. But they can also be spelled—as dictionaries note (and crossword creators often find places in their puzzles for such odd vocables). Thus one may write "a word ending in gee" instead of "a word ending with the letter *g*."

For example, the second letter of our alphabet is spelled "bee." Are the lexically accepted spellings for our English consonants, well, *consonant* with what you'd expect them to be? Maybe not in all cases, but for several of the letters more than one answer is considered correct.

Write in the spelled or word versions of the remaining 20 consonants, from *c* to *z*.

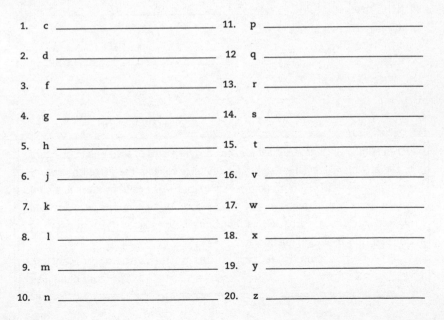

1. c _____   11. p _____

2. d _____   12 q _____

3. f _____   13. r _____

4. g _____   14. s _____

5. h _____   15. t _____

6. j _____   16. v _____

7. k _____   17. w _____

8. l _____   18. x _____

9. m _____   19. y _____

10. n _____ 20. z _____

✿ Five-Word Quizzicles 7–9

The words in each of these wee bees have not been idly chosen.
Write in the correct spelling.

Seven

1. KAK-ee   _____

   (light yellowish brown)

2. GINK-o   _____

   (tree with fan-shaped leaves)

3. GEK-o   _____

   (small lizard)

4. GAHN-dee   _____

   (pacifist leader of India, 1869–1948)

5. GER-kuh   _____

   (Nepalese soldier in the British or Indian army)

When [William] Caxton settled for the idiosyncrasies of the English he heard in the streets of London—"right" for instance reflects the fifteenth-century pronunciation "richt: (ch pronounced as in loch)—he (and printers like him) helped to fix the language on the page before its writers and teachers had reached a consensus. It is to this that English owes some of its chaotic and exasperating spelling conventions.

—Robert McCrum, William Cran, and Robert MacNeil,
The Story of English

Eight

1. sa-SHAY   _____

   (to walk or glide in a mannered or presumptuous way)

2. sa-SHAY   _____

   (small aromatic packet)

3. in-VAY   _____

   (to rail against or rant)

4. dis-TRAY   _____

   (distracted or preoccupied)

5. kor-uh-FAY   _____

   (dancer who is part of a small ballet group)

Nine

1. RACH-uh-tee   _____

   (operating or sounding like a toothed mechanism)

2. KRAH-chuh-tee   _____

   (elderly and cranky)

3. MUK-uh-tee-muk   _____

   (important or self-important person)

4. RIK-uh-tee   _____

   (rundown or shaky)

5. LIK-uh-tee-split   _____

   (with great speed)

❀ Say It and Spell It 3

Write in the correct spelling.

1. de-VWAHRS
    (respects or formal farewell)
    _____

2. kahn-fuh-REE
    (conference participant)
    _____

3. MYOO-suh-lij
    (adhesive substance)
    _____

4. SER-reed
    (dense or crowded)
    _____

5. MYOO-zlee
    (mixed breakfast cereal with dried fruit)
    _____

6. TOOT-lij
    (guardianship, protection, or instruction)
    _____

7. KOO-tor-ee-AYR
    (female high-fashion designer)
    _____

8. swan-YAY
    (elegantly groomed)
    _____

9. SHIF-uh-rohb
    (wardrobe-chest of drawers)
    _____

10. jim-KAH-nuh
    (equestrian games or exhibition)
    _____

11. **duh-SEED-unt** _____

    (dead person)

12. **LUV-ee-DUV-ee** _____

    (very affectionate or suspiciously so)

13. **per-i-puh-TET-ik** _____

    (moving around)

14. **JOO-dee-iz-um** _____

    (Jewish religion or culture)

15. **flo-TIL-uh** _____

    (military fleet)

16. **SHAL-ut** _____

    (green onion)

17. **eks-KUR-sis** _____

    (digression)

18. **fran-juh-PAN-ee** _____

    (tropical American shrub with funnel-shaped flowers)

19. **gal-uh-MO-free** _____

    (hodgepodge)

20. **see-FAHL-uh-jee** _____

    (study of elections)

❋ Word and Definition Match 2

Match each (numbered) word on the left with its correct (lettered) definition on the right. Each numbered word has, also in the left column, a soundalike but differently spelled "mate"—with a different meaning.

1. valence	a. rear of a gun's barrel	_____
2. breech	b. group of a thousand	_____
3. censer	c. cloth or paper smoothing machine	_____
4. immanent	d. chemical number	_____
5. fetor	e. to power using the feet	_____
6. pedal	f. top of an architectural column	_____
7. calender	g. chain or shackle	_____
8. capitol	h. break or rupture	_____
9. imminent	i. women's hats	_____
10. capital	j. time chart	_____
11. millinery	k. separate or individual	_____
12. censor	l. dwelling within	_____
13. discrete	m. stench	_____
14. peddle	n. to sell	_____
15. calendar	o. impending	_____

16.	valance	p.	prudent	_____
17.	fetter	q.	incense container	_____
18.	breach	r.	state legislative building	_____
19.	millenary	s.	short or edgelike drapery	_____
20.	discreet	t.	moral arbiter	_____

❊ Three-Word Quizzicles 21–25

The words in each of these wee bees have not been idly chosen.
Write in the correct spelling.

Twenty-one

1. **KUT-lut** _____

   (slice of meat, often veal, for frying or broiling)

2. **KUT-uh-bul** _____

   (capable of being cut)

3. **kut-uh-BIL-it-ee** _____

   (amount or percentage of marketable meat in an animal carcass)

Twenty-two

1. an-tee-muh-KAS-er   _____

   (small, decorative fabric cover placed on upholstered furniture arms to prevent soiling)

2. muh-KAK   _____

   (Asian short-tailed monkey usually having tufted eyebrows)

3. MIS-tuh-gahg   _____

   (one who guides others being initiated into religious or cult mysteries)

Twenty-three

1. KOO-doo   _____

   (large African antelope having twisted horns)

2. KUD-zoo   _____

   (fast-growing Asian climbing vine)

3. kuh-ZOO   _____

   (tubelike toy musical instrument played by humming to produce a buzzing tone)

Twenty-four

1. PLAK-erd   _____

   (sign posted or carried by a person in public)

2. PLAK-ut   _____

   (designed opening or slit on a skirt or petticoat)

3. PLAK   _____

   (inscribed thin, often metal wall tablet commonly commemorative)

Twenty-five

1. KACH-uh-TOR-ee _____
   (simmered or stewed with tomatoes, herbs, and other seasonings)

2. kuh-KOW _____
   (dried seed of the tree used in making cocoa and chocolate)

3. kak-i-STAHK-ruh-see _____
   (government by the worst people)

❈ Multiple Choice 4

Circle the correct spelling.

1. a. moitey   b. moity   c. moyety   d. moiety
   (one half)

2. a. solfegio   b. sollfegio   c. solfeggio   d. sol'fegio
   (singing sol-fa syllables)

3. a. parallelism   b. parralelism   c. parallellism   d. paralellism
   (analogous direction, correspondence, or resemblance)

4. a. manicle   b. manickle   c. manackle   d. manacle
   (shackle or handcuff)

5. a. bansai   b. banzai   c. bonsai   d. bonsei
   (art of growing dwarf potted plants and trees)

6. a. flibbertigibetty   b. flibbertigibbety   c. flibbertygibbety   d. flibbertigibbetty
   (flighty)

7. **a.** stilleto   **b.** stilletoe   **c.** stiletto   **d.** stilettoe
    (thin dagger)

8. **a.** tynitis   **b.** tinnitus   **c.** tinitus   **d.** tinitis
    (ringing in the ears)

9. **a.** tryseratops   **b.** triseratops   **c.** triceratops   **d.** tryseritops
    (dinosaur with a neck crest and three horns)

10. **a.** phouie   **b.** phooie   **c.** phooey   **d.** fooey
    (expression of rejection)

11. **a.** scurrillous   **b.** scurilous   **c.** scurillous   **d.** scurrilous
    (coarsely abusive)

12. **a.** bathoscaph   **b.** bathyscaphe   **c.** bathyscaff   **d.** bathyscaffe
    (submersible vessel for deep-sea exploration)

13. **a.** Sassquach   **b.** Saskwatch   **c.** Sasquatch   **d.** Sasquotch
    (Bigfoot, the legendary anthropoid creature)

14. **a.** senor   **b.** seignor   **c.** senore   **d.** senhor
    (Portuguese or Brazilian man)

15. **a.** turniquette   **b.** turniquet   **c.** tourniquette   **d.** tourniquet
    (bandage or binding to check bleeding)

16. **a.** falafell   **b.** felafal   **c.** fallafel   **d.** falafel
    (fried patties or balls of chickpeas)

17. **a.** bisextile   **b.** bissestil   **c.** bisextille   **d.** bissextile
    (pertaining to the added day in leap year)

18. **a.** hubbub   **b.** hubub   **c.** hububb   **d.** hubbubb
    (uproar)

19. **a.** laudnum   **b.** lawdinum   **c.** laudanum   **d.** laudinum
    (tincture of opium)

20. **a.** Hugeunot   **b.** Huegenot   **c.** Huguenot   **d.** Heugenot
    (French Protestant of the sixteenth or seventeenth century)

❇ Five-Word Quizzicles 10–12

The words in each of these wee bees have not been idly chosen.
    Write in the correct spelling.

Ten

1. **ap-uh-LOO-suh**   _____
   (rugged North American saddle horse)

2. **sha-puh-RAL**   _____
   (thicket of dwarf trees or shrubs)

3. **pal-uh-MEE-no**   _____
   (cream- or gold-colored horse)

4. **KAL-uh-boos**   _____
   (local jail)

5. **ka-buh-LAIR-o**   _____
   (cavalier or horseman)

Eleven

1. AW-ful   _____

   (viscera and other less choice parts of a butchered animal)

2. FOHK-sul   _____

   (forward part of a ship's upper deck, or forecastle)

3. WAHS-ul   _____

   (hot, spicy Christmastime drink served in a large bowl)

4. DAK-til   _____

   (type of metrical foot in poetry, an accented syllable followed by two unaccented)

5. TRED-ul   _____

   (powering device on a machine activated by pressing the foot)

Twelve

1. DAH-chuhs   _____

   (Russian summer villas or cottages)

2. O-shee-ose   _____

   (futile, pointless, useless, or idle)

3. MIS-ish   _____

   (prim or prudish)

4. kuh-NISH   _____

   (baked or fried roll of dough often stuffed with meat or potato)

5. PY-see-us   _____

   (glossy black, or like pitch)

✿ Two Words or One 2

In English, many two-word expressions eventually acquire a hyphen and ultimately become a single unhyphenated word. (The look of a word is a factor here: *red ink* is not likely to become *redink*.) It's a constant but unpredictable evolution, if one not true of all compound nouns.

Are the substantives below (per most present-day dictionaries) written as two words or as one—currently? You'll doubtless find some of the answers are a bit surprising.

Circle the correct words or word.

1.	key pad	keypad	14. sun dial	sundial
2.	dart board	dartboard	15. lumber yard	lumberyard
3.	pillow case	pillowcase	16. tongue twister	tonguetwister
4.	red shift	redshift	17. land mass	landmass
5.	role model	rolemodel	18. upper hand	upperhand
6.	snuff box	snuffbox	19. fly speck	flyspeck
7.	mess kit	messkit	20. horse laugh	horselaugh
8.	loan word	loanword	21. pit stop	pitstop
9.	pin setter	pinsetter	22. key chain	keychain
10.	place mat	placemat	23. key ring	keyring
11.	leg room	legroom	24. water craft	watercraft
12.	night soil	nightsoil	25. master class	masterclass
13.	river bank	riverbank		

❁ Say It and Spell It 4

Write in the correct spelling.

1. in-TER-kuh-layt

   (to insert or introduce)

   _____

2. fee-on-KET-o

   (chess move developing a bishop)

   _____

3. JON-kwil

   (fragrant flower)

   _____

4. SWEE-bak

   (crispy egg-enriched baked bread)

   _____

5. hi-BAH-chee

   (Japanese-style charcoal brazier)

   _____

6. KAY-san

   (artillery vehicle or watertight chamber)

   _____

7. rap-RAHSH-mahn

   (cordial reconciliation)

   _____

8. uh-PIS-kuh-pit

   (hierarchy of bishops)

   _____

9. sem-pit-ER-nul

   (without end)

   _____

10. SKUT-ul-but

    (rumor or gossip)

    _____

11. **kup-AR-uh-sun** _____

    (colorful covering for a horse)

12. **ahn-truh-MAY** _____

    (dessert or other dishes accompanying the main course)

13. **SHAH-mun** _____

    (tribal priest and seer)

14. **al-uh-PEE-shuh** _____

    (baldness)

15. **SAYN** _____

    (vertically hanging floating fishnet)

16. **DAL-yuh** _____

    (ornamental flower)

17. **ig-nus-FACH-yoo-us** _____

    (deceptive or fatuous hope or purpose)

18. **SHIB-uh-leth** _____

    (distinguishing usage or criterion)

19. **BEL-weth-er** _____

    (leader or indicator)

20. **THER-uh-fer** _____

    (bearer of incense vessel in church)

❀ Three-Word Quizzicles 26–30

The words in each of these wee bees have not been idly chosen.
   Write in the correct spelling.

Twenty-six

1. EYE-let   _____

   (small hole, as for inserting a lace on a garment)

2. EYE-eye   _____

   (small nocturnal primate of Madagascar having long fingers)

3. AG-lit   _____

   (end covering or tag on a lace)

Twenty-seven

1. PET-ee-poynt   _____

   (small stitch used in embroidery)

2. pet-ee-FAHG-uh-ree   _____

   (petty or shifty quibbling, as by an unprincipled lawyer)

3. PAT-ee-kayk   _____

   (nursery game involving claps of the hands and rhymes)

Who cares about spelling? Milton spelt dog with two g's. The American Milton, when he comes, may spell it with three, while all the world wonders, if he is so minded.

—Augustine Birrell

Twenty-eight

1. muh-RANG   _____

   (baked light and frothy sweet topping, as for a pie)

2. muh-REN-gay   _____

   (West Indian ballroom dance)

3. muh-RAYN   _____

   (deposit of rocky, sandy, etc., material left by a glacier)

Twenty-nine

1. ER-uh-thriz-um   _____

   (pronounced or unusual pigmentary redness)

2. ER-uh-thiz-um   _____

   (abnormal, extreme physical response or sensitivity to stimulation)

3. yoo-RITH-me   _____

   (harmony or grace of body movement or of proportions)

Thirty

1. tahr-TER-ee-un   _____

   (pertaining to the infernal or the underworld)

2. tahr-TER-ee-un   _____

   (pertaining to various Mongol tribes; violent in temperament)

3. TAHR-ter-us   _____

   (showing a bacterial deposit on teeth)

❀ Accent Mark or None

They're called loan words or foreign borrowings. Place accent marks (or diacritics) where called for.

1. manana
   (tomorrow)

2. dojo
   (self-defense training school)

3. caique
   (narrow skiff of the Middle East)

4. panache
   (dash and flair)

5. arrividerci
   (good-bye for now)

6. porte cochere
   (passageway to a courtyard)

7. Gotterdammerung
   (catastrophic collapse or disorder)

8. dolce vita
   (the sweet, lazy life)

9. mano a mano
   (head-on, or competing directly)

10. crepe suzette
    (rolled liqueur-sprinkled pancake flambé)

11. **ouzo**

    (Greek anise-flavored liqueur)

12. **zabaglione**

    (Italian dessert sauce)

13. **deja vu**

    (sensation of having experienced something before)

14. **emigre**

    (person departing a country for political reasons)

15. **creche**

    (Nativity scene representation)

16. **lese majeste**

    (affront to those higher up and powerful)

17. **objet d'art**

    (valuable article of art)

18. **apercu**

    (a particular discerning insight)

19. **ciao**

    (hello or good-bye)

20. **gemutlichkeit**

    (friendliness or coziness)

21. **forte**

    (strong point)

22. **kielbasa**
    (Polish sausage)

23. **tete-a-tete**
    (private conversation)

24. **dacha**
    (Russian country cottage)

25. **machismo**
    (masculine preening or posturing)

❈ Multiple Choice 5

Circle the correct spelling.

1. **a.** catachumen   **b.** catechuman   **c.** catechumen   **d.** katachumin
   (one receiving Christian instruction)

2. **a.** mennorah   **b.** menorha   **c.** mennorha   **d.** menorah
   (candelabrum used in Judaism)

3. **a.** caniption   **b.** coniption   **c.** connyption   **d.** conniption
   (angry or hysterical fit)

4. **a.** scentilla   **b.** scintila   **c.** sintilla   **d.** scintilla
   (trace or bit)

5. **a.** fierier   **b.** firier   **c.** fireier   **d.** fieryer
   (having more flammatory power or spirit)

6. **a**. trichinosis   **b**. trychanosis   c. trichanosis   **d**. trychinosis
   (disease from undercooked pork)

7. **a**. malapropo   **b**. malappropo   c. malappropos   **d**. malapropos
   (inappropriate)

8. **a**. milquitoast   **b**. milquetoast   c. milq'toast   **d**. milktoast
   (meek person)

9. **a**. measily   **b**. measley   c. measly   **d**. measelly
   (despicably small)

10. **a**. shillyshallier   **b**. shillishallier   c. shilly-shallier   **d**. shili-shalier
    (one who hesitates, vacillates, or is irresolute)

11. **a**. bralle   **b**. breille   c. braille   **d**. brälle
    (raised-dot touch system for reading by the blind)

12. **a**. deboosh   **b**. debooch   c. debouche   **d**. debouch
    (to emerge or issue out)

13. **a**. centinnary   **b**. centennary   c. centenary   **d**. centenery
    (one-hundredth anniversary; centennial)

14. **a**. boutonier   **b**. bouttonier   c. bouttoniere   **d**. boutonniere
    (buttonhole flower)

15. **a**. sequeli   **b**. sequelae   c. sequellae   **d**. sequelli
    (disease or injury aftereffects)

16. **a**. baccalaureat   **b**. bacchalaureate   c. baccalaureate   **d**. bacchalaureat
    (college bachelor's degree)

17. **a.** poultice   **b.** poltise   **c.** poltice   **d.** poultise
    (warm or medicated substance with a cloth)

18. **a.** glazeer   **b.** glasiere   **c.** glazier   **d.** glaziere
    (window fitter)

19. **a.** annyline   **b.** aniline   **c.** analine   **d.** anniline
    (amine used in dyes)

20. **a.** mearshaum   **b.** meershawm   **c.** meerschaum   **d.** mierschaum
    (white clayey silicate used for tobacco pipes)

❈ One-Syllable Words

Write in the correct spelling.

1. **BANZ** _____
   (public, usually church announcement of an imminent marriage)

2. **SIV** _____
   (perforated straining or draining implement)

3. **KYOO** _____
   (line of people, as before a bank teller's window)

4. **ZIST** _____
   (ancient covered portico or promenade)

5. **BROOM** _____
   (light, enclosed four-wheeled horse carriage)

6. **FLAHKS** _____

   (flowering North American plant)

7. **NOOS** _____

   (mind, intellect, or reason, philosophically)

8. **TOPE** _____

   (brownish gray)

9. **DOW** _____

   (Arab sailing boat having two or three masts)

10. **DROWT** _____

    (climatic period of extreme dryness)

11. **NYS** _____

    (metamorphic rock, often composed of varicolored bands)

12. **MER** _____

    (aromatic gum resin used in incense or perfume)

13. **POOCH** _____

    (plotted overthrow of a government)

14. **NER** _____

    (gnarl, or protuberance on a tree trunk)

15. **KLOHSH** _____

    (close-fitting, bell-shaped woman's hat with a narrow brim)

16. **DAYN** _____

    (to condescend superciliously)

17. **TRIST** _____

    (time and place arranged by lovers to meet)

18. **ROOSH** _____

    (gathered, pleated, etc., strip of fabric for finishing or trimming a garment)

19. **FIZ** _____

    (face or countenance)

20. **SHER** _____

    (to bake until set, as shelled eggs)

21. **LUF** _____

    (to sail closer to the wind)

22. **CONK** _____

    (large mollusk or its spiral-like shell)

23. **TRAWF** _____

    (usually long and open animal feeding receptacle)

24. **KWYR** _____

    (quantity of 24 sheets of paper)

25. **BWAHT** _____

    (nightclub or cabaret)

English spelling is notoriously inconsistent and it is rather hard on those whose only wish is to be left alone that failure to master its intricacies is sometimes regarded as one of the clearest signs of an inadequate education.

—G. L. Brook

❈ Three-Word Quizzicles 31–35

The words in each of these wee bees have not been idly chosen.
Write in the correct spelling.

Thirty-one

1. AHN-iks
   (black or jet black)

   _____

2. AW-ruks
   (European bison)

   _____

3. LUM-uks
   (clumsy or stupid oaf)

   _____

Thirty-two

1. HYOO-mus
   (dark and fertile organic material in soil)

   _____

2. HUH-mus
   (Middle Eastern chickpea-and-sesame paste or dip)

   _____

3. HY-HO
   (exclamation of weariness, boredom, surprise, delight, etc.)

   _____

_Take care that you never spell a word wrong. Always before you write a word,
consider how it is spelled, and, if you do not remember it, turn to a dictionary.
It produces great praise to a lady to spell well._

—Thomas Jefferson

Thirty-three

1. TROO-buh-dor   _____

   (wandering singer-poet of the Middle Ages)

2. MIN-uh-tor   _____

   (in myth, a half-man monster with the head of a bull, confined in a labyrinth)

3. MIN-uh-tor-ee   _____

   (threatening or menacing)

Thirty-four

1. PEK-uh-ree   _____

   (nocturnal piglike hoofed animal of North and South America)

2. pek-AH-wee   _____

   (admission of guilt, sin, or wrongdoing)

3. pe-KYOO-nee-er-ee   _____

   (pertaining to money)

Thirty-five

1. SKAR-ub   _____

   (sacred Egyptian beetle or its likeness as an amulet, cut gem, etc.)

2. KAR-ub   _____

   (chocolate substitute from pods of a Mediterranean tree)

3. kuh-REE-bee   _____

   (piranha, a voracious sharp-toothed small fish)

❁ Say It and Spell It 5

Write in the correct spelling.

1. shuh-KAY-nuh-ree
    (trickery)
    _____

2. sim-PAHT-uh-ko
    (likable as a person)
    _____

3. WIK-ee-up
    (North American Indian frame hut)
    _____

4. koo-LAHT
    (woman's skirtlike pants)
    _____

5. DEP-il-ayt
    (to remove hair)
    _____

6. kul-de-SAK
    (dead-end street)
    _____

7. pol-ee-AN-uh
    (overly optimistic person)
    _____

8. uh-KROO-ul
    (increase or accumulation)
    _____

9. HOOK-uh
    (water pipe, for smoking)
    _____

10. VY-ing
    (contesting)
    _____

11. **pat-ruh-LIN-ee-ul** _____
    (descending from the father)

12. **bib-lee-AHL-uh-ter** _____
    (book or books devotee)

13. **HAYR-breth** _____
    (very narrow margin)

14. **Ef-er-VES-es** _____
    (bubbles)

15. **KER-vuh-cher** _____
    (state of being curved)

16. **kro-SHAY-er** _____
    (practitioner of needlework, using a hooked needle and looped stitches)

17. **tee-lee-AHL-uh-jee** _____
    (study of ultimate purposes or final causes)

18. **PAN-tee-wayst** _____
    (sissy)

19. **tan-TIV-ee** _____
    (at a gallop or at full speed)

20. **TEE-toh-tum** _____
    (small letter-inscribed top used in games)

❋ Five-Word Quizzicles 13–15

The words in each of these wee bees have not been idly chosen.
Write in the correct spelling.

Thirteen

1. fil-ee-o-PY-uh-tiz-um _____

   (veneration of one's ancestors)

2. fil-AT-uh-lee _____

   (stamp collecting)

3. fil-AK-ter-ee _____

   (small scriptural box worn by Orthodox Jews)

4. FIL-up _____

   (extra boost or stimulus)

5. FIL-fut _____

   (swastika)

Tom Sawyer stepped forward with conceited confidence and soared into the unquenchable and indestructible "Give me liberty or give me death" speech, with fine fury and frantic gesticulation, and broke down in the middle of it. . . . Tom struggled a while and then retired, utterly defeated. There was a weak attempt at applause, but it died early.

"The Boy Stood on the Burning Deck" followed; also "The Assyrian Came Down," and other declamatory gems. Then there were reading exercises, and a spelling fight.

—Mark Twain

Fourteen

1. buh-ZOO-kee   _____

   (Greek mandolinlike string instrument with a long neck)

2. ker-FLOO-ee   _____

   ([to go] wrong, collapse, or fall apart)

3. eye-O-lee   _____

   (French garlic-seasoned mayonnaise)

4. sal-muh-GUN-dee   _____

   (large and varied salad plate with meats, vegetables, etc., arranged in rows)

5. uh-GOO-tee   _____

   (rabbit-sized rodent of tropical America)

Fifteen

1. dy-ER-uh-sis   _____

   (double-dot mark over a vowel to indicate that it is pronounced separately)

2. DY-uh-sis   _____

   (double-dagger symbol used as a reference mark in books)

3. DY-uh-sis   _____

   (jurisdiction of a bishop)

4. dy-uh-REE-sus   _____

   (excessive urination)

5. dy-uh-fuh-REE-sis   _____

   (perspiration, especially when excessive or medically caused)

✿ No, No, No—Yes! 1

The three spellings shown for each word below are incorrect. Write in the correct spelling.

1. baccilus   bacilus   baccillus

_____

2. bahtfly   battfly   batfly

_____

3. chasauble   chassible   chasible

_____

4. shmeerkase   schmeerkase   shmierkase

_____

5. keppie   keppi   kepie

_____

6. battik   bottik   batikk

_____

7. wam-pam   wampam   wam-pum

_____

8. nugat   nuggate   nougate

_____

9. tattarsall   tatersall   tattersal

_____

10. yalmulke   yarlmulke   yamulke

_____

11. lachrimose	lacrymose	lacrimose
12. beddizzen	beddizen	bedizzen
13. apparatchick	aparatchik	apparachik
14. croupié	crew-pié	croopier
15. obloquie	obloquey	obloqoy
16. chinziness	chinzyness	chintzyness
17. alliatory	aliatory	alleatory
18. Zanadu	Zanudu	Xannadu
19. beobob	beobobbe	baobbob
20. easell	easle	easal
21. leprechon	leprichon	leprechawn

22.	dispnia	dispnea	dyspnia

23.	antidiluvian	antideluvian	antedeluvian

24.	staffilococcus	staphylacoccus	staphylococcas

25.	eklogue	ecclogue	echlog

❁ Multiple Choice 6

Circle the correct spelling.

1. **a.** pallazzo   **b.** palazzo   **c.** palazo   **d.** pallazo
   (imposing palacelike building)

2. **a.** chitauqua   **b.** chauttalkwa   **c.** chutawkwah   **d.** chautauqua
   (in U.S. history, local or traveling show combining lectures and entertainment)

3. **a.** espadrille   **b.** espedrille   **c.** espodrille   **d.** espedrill
   (flat shoe with a cloth upper)

4. **a.** narcissist   **b.** narscissist   **c.** narsissist   **d.** narscisist
   (self-enamored person)

5. **a.** pariquot   **b.** paraquot   **c.** paraquat   **d.** pariquat
   (type of weed killer)

6. **a.** Nawgahide   **b.** Naugahide   **c.** Naugahyde   **d.** Nawgahyde
   (vinyl-coated fabric)

7. **a.** encription   **b.** incryption   **c.** encryption   **d.** encrypsion
   (encoding)

8. **a.** Cantabridgean   **b.** Cantabridgian   **c.** Cantibrigian   **d.** Cantabrigian
   (student or graduate of Cambridge University)

9. **a.** Sechzuan   **b.** Szechuan   **c.** Seczhuan   **d.** Sczechuan
   (peppery and spicy type of Chinese cooking)

10. **a.** abcize   **b.** abcise   **c.** abbscise   **d.** abscise
    (to cut off)

11. **a.** salaam   **b.** salahm   **c.** saalam   **d.** salamm
    (Eastern bow of respect with the hand held to the forehead)

12. **a.** habeas corpos   **b.** habeas corpus   **c.** habeus corpus   **d.** habeus corpos
    (writ challenging the detention of an individual)

13. **a.** commissery   **b.** commiserry   **c.** comissary   **d.** commissary
    (movie studio lunchroom)

14. **a.** katafalque   **b.** catifalque   **c.** katifalk   **d.** catafalque
    (ornamental tomblike structure)

15. **a.** Afrikanns   **b.** Afrikans   **c.** Afrikaans   **d.** Afrikkans
    (language of South Africa)

16. **a.** paramountcy   **b.** parimountcey   **c.** paramountcey   **d.** parimouncy
    (supremacy)

17. **a.** generallisimo   **b.** génerallisimo   **c.** generalissimo   **d.** generalisimo
    (*army commander in chief*)

18. **a.** balistrade   **b.** balustrade   **c.** ballistrade   **d.** ballustrade
    (*railing with upright curved supports*)

19. **a.** pasell   **b.** pa'cel   **c.** passel   **d.** passle
    (*large number*)

20. **a.** herculian   **b.** herculeian   **c.** herculaean   **d.** herculean
    (*powerful or extraordinary*)

❃ Three-Word Quizzicles 36–40

The words in each of these wee bees have not been idly chosen.
Write in the correct spelling.

Thirty-six

1. kuh-TAHR   _____
   (*inflammation of mucous membranes with secretions*)

2. si-TAHR   _____
   (*plucked, long-necked string instrument of India*)

3. par-TAIR   _____
   (*theater's seating section to the rear of an orchestra*)

Thirty-seven

1. tsoo-NAH-me   _____

   (formidable sea wave caused by a quake or eruption in the sea floor)

2. ZEE-bek   _____

   (three-masted Mediterranean sailing vessel with long bow and stern projections)

3. TSOOK-tsvang   _____

   (chess position in which any move is damaging to oneself)

Thirty-eight

1. ak-SES-uh-bul   _____

   (capable of being approached, reached, contacted, or influenced)

2. uh-SES-uh-bul   _____

   (capable of being valued, measured, or determined financially)

3. uh-SKRY-buh-bul   _____

   (capable or worthy of being attributed to, caused or created by, or identified)

Thirty-nine

1. zgruh-FEE-toh   _____

   (ceramic technique for showing contrasting colors or layers)

2. TAN-juh-lo   _____

   (hybrid citrus fruit that is a cross between a grapefruit and a tangerine)

3. zoo-KET-o   _____

   (skullcap worn by Roman Catholic clergy)

Forty

1. PEL-ij _____
   (covering fur, hair, etc., of a mammal)

2. PEL-ik-ul _____
   (thin membrane, film, or skin)

3. pe-LA-jik _____
   (pertaining to the open sea)

✿ Spell It Out

How good is your word derivation/word history cred? Cred being from credibility, of course. Human impatience in speech is ever a factor in our changing language, especially since the advent of texting and Internet communications, and many of today's most familiar English words are shorter versions of their originals of years back. Such breezy or sporty curtailments are known as clipped forms.

It may be a stretch, but can you supply—and spell correctly—the "complete" words from which these shortenings derive?

1. piano _____
   (keyboard instrument)

2. cab _____
   (taxi)

3. pants _____
   (lower body garment)

4. mob _____
   (large or unruly crowd)

5. gin _____
   (alcoholic beverage)

6. brig _____
   (temporary jail on a ship)

7. razz   _____
   (vocally mock or heckle)

8. wiener   _____
   (frankfurter)

9. synch   _____
   (proper accordance or harmony)

10. bunk   _____
    (nonsense or bull)

11. patter   _____
    (brisk talk or chatter)

12. rum   _____
    (alcoholic liquor favored in warm climates)

13. cinema   _____
    (motion pictures)

14. ad lib   _____
    (to speak or add spontaneously)

15. pub   _____
    (tavern or bar)

16. fax   _____
    (electronic copy transmission)

17. spats   _____
    (gaiter covering the ankle)

18. perk   _____
    (extra or resultant privilege)

19. vet   _____
    (to investigate one's worthiness)

20. modem   _____
    (computer signal-converting device)

❀ Say It and Spell It 6

Write in the correct spelling.

1. BER-dee-ing   _____
   (achieving one under par in golf)

2. KAN-ee-nes   _____
   (shrewdness)

3. STIP-tik

   (checking bleeding)

   _____

4. kar-uh-VEL

   (sailing ship)

   _____

5. ev-uh-NES-ing

   (dissipating)

   _____

6. mer-muh-RAY-shun

   (flock of starlings)

   _____

7. BIV-uh-wak-ing

   (encamping)

   _____

8. UL-yul-ayt

   (to howl or wail)

   _____

9. GRAN-it

   (rock containing quartz)

   _____

10. BIL-it

    (military lodging)

    _____

11. kon-KEE-stuh-dor

    (sixteenth-century Spanish military leader)

    _____

12. DUM-dum

    (hollow-point bullet)

    _____

13. DUM-dum

    (stupid person)

    _____

14. TOE-paz

    (yellowish gem)

    _____

15. O-lee-o

    (hodgepodge)

    _____

16. TIN-ee-nes

    (characteristics or quality of tin)

    _____

17. AWLD-lang-ZYN

    (good old times)

    _____

18. ter-uh-KAHT-uh

    (fired clay used in art and architecture)

    _____

19. LAP-ful

    (something to be cradled against the loins)

    _____

20. duh-RES

    (forcible restraint)

    _____

❖ Spell the Plural

For each of the following singulars, what is the plural form of the word?

Singular	Plural
1. auto-da-fé _(burning of a heretic)_	_____

Singular	Plural
2. paterfamilias *(male head of a family or household)*	_____
3. court-martial *(military trial)*	_____
4. heir apparent *(presumed inheritor)*	_____
5. quorum *(required number of members present)*	_____
6. stasis *(state of no change)*	_____
7. billet-doux *(love letter)*	_____
8. coccyx *(end of spinal column)*	_____
9. annus mirabilis *(wondrous year)*	_____
10. kohlrabi *(thick-stemmed cabbage)*	_____
11. women's room *(restroom for females)*	_____
12. klezmer *(Jewish folk musician)*	_____

	Singular	Plural

13. bel-esprit
(bright and witty person)

14. pince-nez
(nose-clip eyeglasses)

15. metastasis
(secondary malignant growth)

16. mot juste
(the perfectly apt word)

17. goosefoot
(herb with greenish flowers)

18. manservant
(valet)

19. oyez
("Hear!" cry uttered three times in courtrooms)

20. chassis
(automobile body frame)

21. beau geste
(noble gesture)

22. nouveau riche
(newly rich person)

23. soliloquy
(dramatic monologue)

Singular	Plural
24. bête noire	_____
(something or somebody dreaded or avoided)	
25. modus operandi	_____
(characteristic working method or pattern)	

❋ Three-Word Quizzicles 41–45

The words in each of these wee bees have not been idly chosen.
Write in the correct spelling.

Forty-one

1. PEE-ko   _____
   (Asian type of black tea)

2. FER-buh-lo   _____
   (ornamental detail, bit of trim, or touch of finery on a garment)

3. GEE-o   _____
   (flat-topped seamount on the ocean floor)

Another cause . . . which hath contributed not a little to the maiming of our Language, is a foolish Opinion, advanced of late Years, that we ought to spell exactly as we speak, which beside the obvious Inconvenience of utterly destroying our Etymology, would be a thing we should never see an End of.
      —Jonathan Swift

Forty-two

1. SOO-uh-bul   _____

   (liable or vulnerable to civil-action proceedings)

2. sub-DOO-uh-bul   _____

   (capable of being overcome or conquerable)

3. per-SOO-uh-bul   _____

   (followable, attempt-worthy, or chasable)

Forty-three

1. huh-BIL-uh-ments   _____

   (clothing or dress, especially for a particular occasion)

2. hee-pee-HAH-puh   _____

   (tropical plant from whose leaves Panama hats are made)

3. HIP-it-ee-HAHP   _____

   (in a hopping motion)

Forty-four

1. OR-uh-ree   _____

   (apparatus, with movable orbs and a clock mechanism, showing the motions and relative positions of solar system bodies)

2. OR-uh-flam   _____

   (banner or standard used as a rallying symbol or to inspire)

3. OR-duh-nuns   _____

   (arrangement or harmony of parts in a structure, artistic work, etc.)

Forty-five

1. KLIP-uh-tee-KLAHP   _____

   (characteristic horse's-hoofs sounds, as on a pavement)

2. HAR-um-SKAR-um   _____

   (wild, reckless, or unpredictable)

3. NIM-in-ee PIM-in-ee   _____

   (affectedly refined, fussy, or delicate)

❋ Multiple Choice 7

Circle the correct spelling.

1. a. ciceronne   b. cicerrone   c. ciccerone   d. cicerone
   (tourists' guide)

2. a. inamorata   b. inamouratta   c. enamorata   d. inamoratta
   (woman one loves)

3. a. sebbaceous   b. sebaceous   c. sebbhaceous   d. sebacious
   (fatty)

4. a. crannie   b. cranny   c. cranney   d. craney
   (small crevice)

5. a. collosal   b. colossal   c. collossal   d. colossall
   (gigantic)

6. a. terete   b. turrete   c. turete   d. terrete
   (somewhat cylindrical but with tapered ends)

7. **a.** gutta-percha   **b.** gutta-pertcha   **c.** guta-purcha   **d.** gutta-purcha
    (rubberlike substance used in dentistry)

8. **a.** yturbium   **b.** ytterbium   **c.** yterrbium   **d.** yterbium
    (soft and silvery rare-earth element, atomic number 50)

9. **a.** silouhette   **b.** sillouhette   **c.** sillhouette   **d.** silhouette
    (outline or shaped likeness)

10. **a.** gluttenous   **b.** gluttinous   **c.** glutenous   **d.** glutinous
    (containing doughy protein substance found in wheat flour)

11. **a.** brumagemm   **b.** brummagem   **c.** brummegem   **d.** brumagem
    (cheap or counterfeit)

12. **a.** pennicilin   **b.** peniccilin   **c.** penicillin   **d.** penicilin
    (mold-produced antibiotic)

13. **a.** hors d'oeuvres   **b.** hor d'ouvres   **c.** hor d'oeuvres   **d.** hors d'ouvres
    (appetizers)

14. **a.** syllabary   **b.** syllibary   **c.** sybbilury   **d.** syllabarry
    (list or table of syllables)

15. **a.** gallosches   **b.** galloshes   **c.** galoshes   **d.** galosches
    (high rubber overshoes)

16. **a.** zigurat   **b.** zigurrat   **c.** ziggurat   **d.** ziggurrat
    (ancient pyramidal structure with exterior terraced levels)

17. **a.** iscicle   **b.** iciccle   **c.** icycle   **d.** icicle
    (shaft of ice formed by dripping)

18. **a.** tam-o'-shanter   **b.** tamm-o'-shanter   **c.** tam'-o-shanter   **d.** tam-o-shanter
    (Scottish flat woolen cap with a pom-pom atop)

19. **a.** tryvette   **b.** trivet   **c.** trivette   **d.** tryvet
    (metal support for a hot dish)

20. **a.** succotache   **b.** sucotash   **c.** succotash   **d.** succotasch
    (dish of cooked beans and corn)

❄ Five-Word Quizzicles 16–18

The words in each of these wee bees have not been idly chosen.
Write in the correct spelling.

Sixteen

1. **HIM-nuh-dee** _____
   (the singing or composing of religious songs)

2. **SWAHV-uh-tee** _____
   (smooth, courteous, urbane poise)

3. **KWIK-suh-tree** _____
   (gallant but unrealistic idealism or romanticism)

4. **LAY-uh-tee** _____
   (religious followers or members, as distinct from clergy)

5. **KAHM-uh-tee** _____
   (general or international civility, harmony, or mutual respect)

Seventeen

1. eye-SAHS-tuh-see   _____

   (deviation from the normal)

2. eye-SAHS-uh-lees   _____

   (describing a triangle two of whose sides are equal)

3. ANG-luh-see   _____

   (in English, or in its English form)

4. loo-TEN-un-see   _____

   (the rank, office, or authority of a lieutenant)

5. PEE-kon-see   _____

   (quality of being pleasantly sharp or stimulating)

Eighteen

1. uh-LIK-ser   _____

   (cure-all; panacea)

2. PIN-uh-for   _____

   (child's apron or woman's apronlike dress)

3. AH-vuh-tar   _____

   (Hindu deity's incarnation or an embodiment of something)

4. SEM-uh-for   _____

   (position-changing device for or a method of visual signaling)

5. pah-lee-HIS-tor   _____

   (person of prodigious and extensive learning)

❉ No, No, No—Yes! 2

The three spellings shown for each word below are incorrect. Write in the correct spelling.

1. cicitrix   ciccitrix   ciccatrix

_____

2. discumbobbulate   discombobbulate   discumbobulate

_____

3. oliandor   olliander   olleander

_____

4. divvigation   divvagation   divigation

_____

5. hebdommidal   hebbdomidal   hebdomidal

_____

6. euchalyptus   eucalyptis   euchalyptus

_____

7. shi-shi   chih-chih   chi-chi

_____

8. batallion   battallion   bataillon

_____

9. drommadary   drommedary   dromidary

_____

10. astrakkan   astrekkan   astrakan

_____

11. inveigel   invaigle   invaygle

12. molassis   mollasis   mollasses

13. enthememe   enthomeme   enthymime

14. pasturise   pastorize   pasteurise

15. toopello   toupelo   tuppelo

16. mareschino   marraschino   marreschino

17. terazzo   terazo   turrazzo

18. phantesmagouria   fantesmagouria   fantasmagoria

19. Taggalog   Tagalogg   Taggalogue

20. giggalo   jigalo   jigolo

21. meinad   mynad   maenade

22.	nargyle	nargile	narrgile

23.	rivetment	revettment	rivetement

24.	crysalis	chrysallis	chrysalice

25.	anice	annice	annise

✿ Say It and Spell It 7

Write in the correct spelling.

1. **IS-mus**
   (connecting strip of land)
   _____

2. **pas-par-TOO**
   (master key)
   _____

3. **hy-MEN-ee-ul**
   (nuptial)
   _____

4. **TIZ-ik**
   (tubercular)
   _____

5. **bee-LEEG-er-munt**
   (besieging or harassing)
   _____

6. **BAY-ted** _____

   (reduced or restrained)

7. **ka-FEEN** _____

   (mild alkaloid stimulant)

8. **uh-KROO-munt** _____

   (increase or accumulation)

9. **stay-TOL-uh-tree** _____

   (belief in powerful central government)

10. **ZOM-bee-is-um** _____

    (cult of the living dead)

11. **SHOO-fly** _____

    (molasses–brown sugar mixture used for pie)

12. **uh-BUT-ment** _____

    (projection or architectural support)

13. **AK-need** _____

    (having inflamed skin)

14. **MY-ty** _____

    (cocktail with rum, curacao, and fruit juices)

15. **guh-LOOT** _____

    (odd fellow)

16. **SKLAFF** _____

    (in golf, to scrape the ground on one's swing)

17. **WEJ-wood** _____
    (English ceramic manufacturer)

18. **MIS-ul-ree** _____
    (arsenal of projectiles)

19. **day-kul-TAHJ** _____
    (low neckline)

20. **HAW-zer** _____
    (thick nautical rope)

❀ Three-Word Quizzicles 46–50

The words in each of these wee bees have not been idly chosen.
  Write in the correct spelling.

Forty-six

1. **PEER-ik** _____
   (describing victory or success gained at great or tragic cost)

2. **PY-bald** _____
   (having usually black and white spots or patches, especially a horse)

3. **PEER-glas** _____
   (tall mirror, often one set between two windows)

Forty-seven

1. TRAYPS   _____

   (to tramp or wander about)

2. DAY-is   _____

   (raised platform for a lecturer, speaker, etc.)

3. JAYPS   _____

   (jokes or pranks)

Forty-eight

1. o-POSS-um   _____

   (nocturnal thick-haired marsupial with a long tail)

2. NOY-sum   _____

   (having a foul or putrid odor)

3. KRIS-um   _____

   (nether area of a bird beneath the tail)

Forty-nine

1. FIL-uh-syd   _____

   (murder of a son or daughter, or such a murderer)

2. FY-ul   _____

   (shiny, slightly ribbed woven fabric of silk, rayon, or cotton)

3. FY-ul   _____

   (vial or small container for a liquid)

Fifty

1. **TON-do**
   _____
   (round painting or other artwork)

2. **TOOR-nuh-do**
   _____
   (fillet of tenderloin beef often wrapped in bacon)

3. **RON-do**
   _____
   (brief lyrical poem using two rhymes and an opening repeated twice as a refrain)

❋ -Ious or -Eous

Which of these adjectives are misspelled?

1. nacreous
2. rampagious
3. rambunctious
4. efficacious
5. deletereous
6. contumacious
7. igneous
8. beautious
9. consanguineous
10. extranious
11. veraceous
12. obsequeous
13. vitrious
14. ignomineous
15. Cretaceous

> The dictionary emphasizes the trivial matters of language at the expense of what is truly important. The precise spelling of a word is relatively trivial because no matter how the word is spelled, it nevertheless remains only an approximation of the spoken word. *A machine chose the chords* is a correctly spelled English sentence, but what is written as *ch* is spoken with the three different sounds heard in the words *sheen, catch,* and *kiss.*
>
> —Peter Farb

❁ Multiple Choice 8

Circle the correct spelling.

1. **a.** kolrabbe   **b.** kolrabi   **c.** kohlrabi   **d.** kohlrabe
    (type of cabbage)

2. **a.** philogeny   **b.** philogyny   **c.** phylogyny   **d.** phylogeny
    (evolution of related organisms)

3. **a.** acedophilus   **b.** acidophilus   **c.** acidophyllis   **d.** acidofillus
    (healthful bacterial part of yogurt)

4. **a.** semaphore   **b.** semmiphore   **c.** semiphore   **d.** semmaphor
    (system for signaling by waving of flags)

5. **a.** picallily   **b.** piccalili   **c.** piccallili   **d.** piccalilli
    (relish made from vegetables and spices)

6. **a.** glokenspiel   **b.** glockenspiel   **c.** glockinspiel   **d.** glockanspiel
    (bell-like percussion instrument played with two light hammers)

7. **a.** Drammamine   **b.** Dramamin   **c.** Dramamine   **d.** Drammamin
    (antinausea medication)

8. **a.** doilie   **b.** doily   **c.** doilly   **d.** doillie
    (decorative napkinlike mat)

9. **a.** callomine   **b.** calimine   **c.** calamine   **d.** calomine
    (healing ointment)

10. **a.** tergiversate   **b.** turgiversate   **c.** turjiversate   **d.** terrgiversate
    (to desert a cause or be evasive)

11. **a.** talcy ·   **b.** talcky   **c.** talcey   **d.** talckey
    (having or like a soft silicate used in powder)

12. **a.** ippicac   **b.** ipicac   **c.** ipecac   **d.** ipeccac
    (root used medicinally)

13. **a.** bludgen   **b.** bludgion   **c.** blugeon   **d.** bludgeon
    (to strike in a heavy or brutal way)

14. **a.** poinsetta   **b.** poyntsetta   **c.** pointsettia   **d.** poinsettia
    (Mexican plant having bright red or white bracts)

15. **a.** terpsikorean   **b.** terpsichorian   **c.** terpsichorean   **d.** terpsicorian
    (pertaining to dance or dancing)

16. **a.** afidavit   **b.** affidavid   **c.** afidavitt   **d.** affidavit
    (legalized sworn statement)

17. **a.** hemmorage   **b.** hemorrhage   **c.** hemmhorage   **d.** hemorhage
    (extreme bleeding)

18. **a.** capuccino   **b.** cappucino   **c.** cappuccino   **d.** capucino
    (espresso with steamed milk or cream)

19. **a.** Capouchin   **b.** Cappuchin   **c.** Capuchin   **d.** Caputchin
    (member of an austere Franciscan monastic order)

20. **a.** obelisk   **b.** obbelisk   **c.** obelisque   **d.** obbelisque
    (squared and tapering pillarlike monument)

❊ Five-Word Quizzicles 19–21

The words in each of these wee bees have not been idly chosen.
  Write in the correct spelling.

Nineteen

1. in-VAY-gul   _____
   (to persuade artfully or with flattery)

2. ah-LAY   _____
   (long walkway lined with trees)

3. HWAY-faced   _____
   (pallid)

4. HAY-day   _____
   (one's prime or a period of greatest success, notability, etc.)

5. doo-VAY   _____
   (quilt or comforter)

Even in so settled a matter as spelling, a dictionary cannot always be absolute. . . . The reader may want a single certainty. He may have taken an unyielding position in an argument, he may have wagered in support of his conviction and may demand that the dictionary "settle" the matter. But neither his vanity nor his purse is any concern of the dictionary's; it must record the facts. And the fact here is that there are many words in our language which may be spelled, with equal correctness, in either of two ways.

—Bergen Evans and Cornelia Evans

Twenty

1. port-KUL-is _____

   (raisable iron grating at gateway of a medieval fortification)

2. TREL-is _____

   (supportive frame for plants or vines)

3. RIK-tus _____

   (gapingly pronounced or macabre grin or grimace)

4. KRIS-uh-lis _____

   (emergent butterfly's pupa or protective covering)

5. KAHK-uh-tris _____

   (legendary serpentine monster having a deadly glance)

Twenty-one

1. SPIL-way _____

   (passage or outlet at a dam, lake, etc., for overflow water)

2. BUL-werk _____

   (defensive wall or rampart)

3. BEL-free _____

   (tower or steeple having a bell or bells)

4. HEL-uh-tree _____

   (slavery or serfdom)

5. MIL-ee-er-ee _____

   (having bumps, lesions, or blisters like millet seeds)

✿ Mega Multiple Choice

In a test, can eight spelling options instead of the usual two, three, or four make certainty (or correct answers) even harder?

Which of the spellings below for each word is the single correct one?

1. *(in music, a preceding embellishing note)*
   a. apoggiatura   b. apagiatura   c. appogiatura   d. appagiatura
   e. apogeatura   f. appoggiatura   g. apaggiatura   h. appaggiatura

2. *(constellation between Andromeda and Cepheus)*
   a. Casciopiea   b. Casiopia   c. Casiopaea   d. Casseopea
   e. Cassiopeia   f. Cassiopaeia   g. Casioppia   h. Cassiopia

3. *(acute skin disease)*
   a. errysipolis   b. erisipylos   c. erisippelas   d. erysipelas
   e. erysippilas   f. erisypilus   g. erysypoles   h. errisipulos

4. *(Greek god of fire and metalworking)*
   a. Hephaestus   b. Hephestos   c. Hephaestos   d. Haephestos
   e. Haephestus   f. Hephestus   g. Hephestis   h. Haephaestus

5. *(obtusely and fundamentally dense or stupid)*
   a. beoshian   b. beotean   c. beoetian   d. boeoshian
   e. boeotian   f. beocean   g. beoshean   h. boeocian

6. *(Japanese ritual suicide; hara-kiri)*
   a. sepukku   b. seppuku   c. sepoukkou   d. seppukku
   e. sepukkue   f. seppoukou   g. sepuku   h. sepukue

7. *(pigment in bile and blood an excess of which can cause jaundice)*

   a. bilyrubin   **b.** billirubin   **c.** billirueben   **d.** bilyrubbin

   e. billireuben   **f.** billyruben   **g.** bilirubin   **h.** bylliruben

8. *(on a column, an outward curve connecting the shaft with the base)*

   a. apopthagee   **b.** apopthage   **c.** apopfogee   **d.** apophyge

   e. aphophyge   **f.** appophogy   **g.** appophage   **h.** appophyge

9. *(ancient time-measuring device, a water clock)*

   a. klepseidra   **b.** clepsydra   **c.** cleppseidra   **d.** kleppseidra

   e. klepsydra   **f.** clepsidra   **g.** clepssydra   **h.** klepssydra

10. *(a substitute)*

    a. sucsidanium   **b.** succidanium   **c.** sucsedanium   **d.** succedaneum

    e. sucsedaneum   **f.** succidaneum   **g.** suksidanium   **h.** sukksidanium

❊ Three-Word Quizzicles 51–55

The words in each of these wee bees have not been idly chosen.
Write in the correct spelling.

Fifty-one

1. **tar-BOOSH**   _____

   (tasseled cloth or felt cap worn by a male Muslim)

2. **fuh-ROOSH**   _____

   (wild or feral)

3. **ruh-GOO**   _____

   (stew of seasoned meat or fish and often vegetables)

Fifty-two

1. KROO

    _____

    (classification or grade of wine or the vineyard producing it)

2. KROOS

    _____

    (earthenware jar, pot, or bottle for liquids)

3. KROO

    _____

    (private club of paraders in the New Orleans Mardi Gras carnival)

Fifty-three

1. PEEZ-uh-lay

    _____

    (last resort)

2. pee-uh-ZOM-uh-ter

    _____

    (pressure-measuring instrument)

3. SPEE-shee

    _____

    (coined money)

Fifty-four

1. AK-ak

    _____

    (antiaircraft fire)

2. BRIK-uh-brak

    _____

    (collection of small decorative or sentimental objects)

3. DIK-dik

    _____

    (small African antelope)

Fifty-five

1. **TER-muh-gent** _____

   (shrewish or scolding woman)

2. **UN-gwent** _____

   (soothing ointment or salve)

3. **VY-kownt** _____

   (nobleman ranking above a baron and below an earl)

❇ Say It and Spell It 8

Write in the correct spelling.

1. **SEM-uh-nul** _____

   (centrally indispensable, creative)

2. **DAM-fool** _____

   (unbelievably dumb or unwise)

3. **kuh-MEM-uh-rayt** _____

   (to honor in memory)

4. **PLAY-ryt** _____

   (dramatist)

5. **uh-NOYNT** _____

   (to bedaub with oil or consecrate)

6. **duh-FER-muhnt**

   (postponement)

   _____

7. **STOO-puh-fy**

   (to bewilder)

   _____

8. **ek-so-THAL-mik**

   (having prominent eyeballs)

   _____

9. **SEKT**

   (German champagne)

   _____

10. **kon-sen-TAY-nee-us**

    (in agreement or unanimous)

    _____

11. **VIT-ree-ul**

    (acid, caustic antipathy)

    _____

12. **kon-FER-ul**

    (bestowal or consultation)

    _____

13. **RIV-yoo-let**

    (small stream)

    _____

14. **LIN-tul**

    (horizontal span or support)

    _____

15. **uh-PYEWN**

    (to assail)

    _____

16. **WAWL-les**

    (lacking a vertical enclosure or partition)

    _____

17. **GUT-uh-rul**
    (from the throat)

    _____

18. **OW-let**
    (small owl)

    _____

19. **AHR-muh-cher**
    (framework)

    _____

20. **FRESH-et**
    (stream overflow)

    _____

❁ -Ie or -Ei

Complete the correct spelling by filling in the space with *ie* or *ei*.

1. w _____ rd
2. sh _____ kh
3. f _____ nd
4. sk _____ n
5. fr _____ ze
6. dec _____ ve
7. s _____ ze
8. forf _____ t
9. g _____ sha

10. w _____ r
11. cod _____ ne
12. caff _____ ne
13. s _____ ve
14. s _____ ge
15. c _____ ling
16. f _____ fdom
17. w _____ ld
18. conc _____ ve

19. rec _____ pt
20. retr _____ ve
21. n _____ ce
22. S _____ gfr _____ d line
23. k _____ lbasa
24. l _____ der
25. h _____ nous

❀ Multiple Choice 9

Circle the correct spelling.

1. **a.** fatic   **b.** phatic   **c.** phattic   **d.** fattic
   (pertaining to speech that is sociable rather than communicating information)

2. **a.** tinntinnabulation   **b.** tintinabulation   **c.** tinntinabulation   **d.** tintinnabulation
   (ringing or chiming)

3. **a.** placket   **b.** plaquet   **c.** plackette   **d.** plackit
   (slit in a garment)

4. **a.** daguerreotype   **b.** daguerotype   **c.** degeurrotype   **d.** daguerriotype
   (old photograph on a silver or copper plate)

5. **a.** rutabaga   **b.** rootabaga   **c.** rootibaga   **d.** rutibaga
   (type of turnip)

6. **a.** sveldtness   **b.** svelltness   **c.** svelteness   **d.** sveltness
   (state of being appealingly slim or slender)

7. **a.** foie gras   **b.** fois gras   **c.** foi gràce   **d.** foisgras
   (pâté, especially of goose liver)

8. **a.** geniollogically   **b.** genealogically   **c.** genealogicly   **d.** geniologically
   (in terms of family or heredity)

9. **a.** panagyric   **b.** panegyric   **c.** pannagyric   **d.** panogyric
   (speech of praise; encomium)

10. **a.** tatterdamalion   **b.** tatterdemalion   **c.** tatterdemaleon   **d.** tatterdamaleon
    (ragamuffin)

11. **a.** bicentennary   **b.** bicentenary   **c.** bicentinary   **d.** bicentenery
    (two-hundredth anniversary; bicentennial)

12. **a.** mallette   **b.** mallet   **c.** malette   **d.** mallett
    (hammer with a wooden head)

13. **a.** abbacuses   **b.** abbaccuses   **c.** abacusses   **d.** abacuses
    (calculating instruments using movable beads on rods)

14. **a.** rimy   **b.** rhimy   **c.** rhimey   **d.** rimey
    (frosty)

15. **a.** shakkra   **b.** chakra   **c.** chakkra   **d.** shakra
    (in yoga, one of the human body's seven centers of energy)

16. **a.** Antiaen   **b.** Antean   **c.** Antaean   **d.** Anteian
    (having superhuman strength)

17. **a.** litoral   **b.** litteral   **c.** littoral   **d.** litorral
    (coastline)

18. **a.** acetyleen   **b.** ascetylene   **c.** accetylene   **d.** acetylene
    (hydrocarbon used in welding)

19. **a.** catanary   **b.** katanary   **c.** katenary   **d.** catenary
    (chainlike)

20. **a.** fedorah   **b.** fadorah   **c.** fadorra   **d.** fedora
    (man's low soft felt hat with a flexible brim)

❋ Three-Word Quizzicles 56–60

The words in each of these wee bees have not been idly chosen.
    Write in the correct spelling.

Fifty-six

1. PLIM-sul (~ mark or ~ line)   _____

    (load or depth lines on a hull indicating the weight of a merchant ship's cargo)

2. pis-TOHL   _____

    (former Spanish gold coin equal to two escudos)

3. puh-ROHL   _____

    (utterance or something stated orally)

Fifty-seven

1. AN-nyl   _____

    (old-womanish)

2. en-NYL   _____

    (to place on an island or to isolate)

3. EE-nuh-fyl   _____

    (wine lover or connoisseur)

> Good spelling enhances your attractiveness in social life and in your career.
> Good spelling facilitates studying and increases your chances of getting and
> holding a responsible job. And, after all, learning to spell well isn't as hard as
> you might think.
>
> —Edna L. Furness

Fifty-eight

1. bel-LET-rist   _____

   (writer of aesthetically fine, light, or sophisticated prose)

2. bel-KON-toh   _____

   (operatic vocal style that is graceful and flowing)

3. bel-uh-DON-uh   _____

   (deadly nightshade, a poisonous herb)

Fifty-nine

1. MY-kro-feesh   _____

   (sheet of microfilm bearing pages of printed text)

2. KEESH   _____

   (nonsweet custard pie with cheese, vegetable, etc., ingredients)

3. BAK-sheesh   _____

   (tip or bribe, especially in the Middle East)

Sixty

1. KWERT   _____

   (short-handled riding whip)

2. KWER-tee   _____

   (standard typewriter or computer keyboard configuration)

3. kwi-RAS   _____

   (upper-body or torso-protective article of armor)

❀ British Spelling

As the immortal quote goes, we Americans and the United Kingdom are "separated by a common language." Not only do the British have words thoroughly alien to us (knackered, swingeing, gormless, and all those one-syllable epithets from bloke, nob, and git to ponce, toff, and twit), they sometimes spell words differently—or accuse us of doing so.

Write in the British spellings for these words.

1. eon _____
2. hemorrhage _____
3. curb _____
4. specialty _____
5. pajamas _____
6. pretense _____
7. maneuver _____
8. anemic _____
9. annex _____
10. favorite _____

11. analyze _____
12. counselor _____
13. aluminum _____
14. smolder _____
15. wagon _____
16. furor _____
17. connection _____
18. harbor _____
19. enrollment _____
20. licorice _____

> *Correct spelling is aided by a photographic memory and some familiarity with etymology, especially Latin and Greek. Misspelling is a not innocuous disease against which writers should inoculate themselves with a potion of Latin and Greek roots and regular checkups at Dr. Webster's, the best resort for a spell.*
>
> —John B. Bremner

❁ Five-Word Quizzicles 22–24

The words in each of these wee bees have not been idly chosen.
   Write in the correct spelling.

Twenty-two

1. JA-luh-see   _____
   (shutter, blind, or window with adjustable slats)

2. sin-AHN-uh-me   _____
   (list denoting or differentiating words of like or close meaning)

3. KAHKS-kohm-ree   _____
   (foppish vanity, conceit, or ostentatiousness)

4. fuh-SEE-she-ee   _____
   (lightly witty writings)

5. nuh-PEN-thee   _____
   (supposed potion or concoction that causes forgetfulness)

---

orthography: *The science of spelling by the eye instead of the ear. Advocated with more heat than light by the outmates of every asylum for the insane. They have had to concede a few things since the time of Chaucer, but are none the less hot in defence of those to be conceded hereafter.*

—Ambrose Bierce

Twenty-three

1. BIN-uh-kul _____

   (upright housing for a ship's compass)

2. MIS-ul _____

   (book of prayers or priestly rites)

3. DAHT-ul _____

   (half-smoked tobacco residue in the bowl of a pipe)

4. WEE-vul _____

   (snouted beetle destructive to certain nuts, fruits, grains, etc.)

5. GAM-brul [~ roof] _____

   (two-sided roof with shallower slopes above the deeper ones)

Twenty-four

1. TEN-un _____

   (insertable projection made on a piece of timber)

2. SPAW-run _____

   (Scottish pouch worn at the front of a kilt)

3. RAHZ-in _____

   (hard translucent resin used to rub on the bow of a violin)

4. TAN-in _____

   (sharp-tasting compound used in clarifying red wine)

5. GER-dun _____

   (reward)

❊ Say It and Spell It 9

Write in the correct spelling.

1. **duh-ZERTS**
   (deserved reward or rewards) _____

2. **muh-RID-ee-un-al**
   (southern) _____

3. **kuh-MES-tuh-bul**
   (edible) _____

4. **ob-STREP-uh-rus**
   (unruly) _____

5. **kon-SEN-shoo-ul**
   (by agreement) _____

6. **in-TEN-dens**
   (management or supervision) _____

7. **PIT-ence**
   (small amount) _____

8. **PLOO-mee**
   (like a plume) _____

9. **SHOOD**
   (driven or scared away) _____

10. **AV-uh-lanch**
    (mountain downslide) _____

11. pro-TEM
    (for the time being)

    _____

12. DIV-eed
    (divided)

    _____

13. in-fin-it-ES-i-mul
    (minute in size)

    _____

14. suh-RAHR-ul
    (sisterly)

    _____

15. FAY-uh-ten
    (carriage or touring car)

    _____

16. LENZ-les
    (lacking a piece of curved optical glass)

    _____

17. fyoo-NEER-ee-ul
    (somber)

    _____

18. PAR-uh-syd
    (killing of one's father or such a killer)

    _____

19. HAYR-braynd
    (stupid)

    _____

20. SIN-jer
    (one who singes)

    _____

❋ -Ance or -Ence / -Ant or -Ent

Complete the correct spelling by filling in the space with *a* or *e*.

1. aberr __ nce
2. suffer __ nce
3. resplend __ nt
4. imped __ nce
5. cogniz __ nt
6. despond __ nt
7. petul __ nce
8. conniv __ nce
9. anteced __ nt
10. relev __ nt
11. subsist __ nce
12. opul __ nce
13. dalli __ nce
14. admitt __ nce
15. lieuten __ nt
16. intermitt __ nt
17. attract __ nt
18. decad __ nt
19. deced __ nt
20. defend __ nt
21. pench __ nt
22. preponder __ nt
23. retard __ nt
24. disput __ nt
25. adher __ nt

❋ Three-Word Quizzicles 61–65

The words in each of these wee bees have not been idly chosen.
Write in the correct spelling.

Sixty-one

1. MER-lun _____

   (solid, rectilinear toothlike part of a battlement)

2. GY-don _____

   (pennant carried in the military as a unit designator)

3. MID-un _____

   (refuse heap or dunghill)

Sixty-two

1. BAYZ

   _____

   (usually green, feltlike fabric used as the surface of billiard tables)

2. kahk-AYN

   _____

   (imaginary land or paradise of ease and luxury)

3. payn-WAHR

   _____

   (woman's loose dressing gown)

Sixty-three

1. FET-uh-kom-PLEE

   _____

   (acts or events done or achieved and irreversible)

2. FET-or

   _____

   (stench)

3. fet-shom-PET-ruh

   _____

   (outdoor celebration or garden party)

Sixty-four

1. PIJ-un

   _____

   (short-legged, stout-bodied bird often abundant in towns or cities)

2. STI-jee-un

   _____

   (infernally dark and gloomy)

3. mis-PRI-zhun

   _____

   (wrongful or neglectful performance of duty in public office)

Sixty-five

1. MYOOL   _____
   (to cry weakly or whimper)

2. PYOOL   _____
   (to whine or whimper)

3. SHOOL   _____
   (synagogue)

✸ Multiple Choice 10

Circle the correct spelling

1. a. noctalopia   b. nyctilopia   c. nyctalopia   d. nictolopia
   (night blindness)

2. a. adinoidal   b. adynoidal   c. adenoidal   d. adynnoidal
   (pertaining to tissue at the back of the pharynx)

3. a. chameleon   b. camelion   c. camellion   d. chamellion
   (lizard whose skin changes color)

4. a. archepellago   b. archipelago   c. archipellago   d. archepelago
   (area of the sea having many islands)

5. a. bougainvillea   b. bouganvillea   c. bougainvillia   d. bougaenvillia
   (colorful American tropical woody vine)

6. a. prestidigitater b. prestidigitator c. prestodigitater d. prestydigitator
   (sleight-of-hand artist)

7. **a.** spinate   **b.** spinet   **c.** spinette   **d.** spinnet
   (small upright piano)

8. **a.** uskwebogh   **b.** usquebaugh   **c.** usquiboggh   **d.** uskwebawgh
   (whiskey)

9. **a.** brisket   **b.** briskette   **c.** brisquet   **d.** brisquette
   (breast cut of beef)

10. **a.** demurrhal   **b.** demurhal   **c.** demurral   **d.** demerral
    (hesitation or objection)

11. **a.** mineret   **b.** minerette   **c.** minaret   **d.** minarette
    (slender mosque tower)

12. **a.** homburg   **b.** hamborg   **c.** hamburg   **d.** homberg
    (man's felt hat with a curled brim)

13. **a.** borborrigmus   **b.** borborigmus   **c.** borborygmus   **d.** borberigmus
    (internal rumblings of intestinal gas)

14. **a.** passamentery   **b.** passementerie   **c.** passimenterie   **d.** passimentery
    (fancy trimming or edging)

15. **a.** ethnogeny   **b.** ethnogony   **c.** ethnogyny   **d.** ethnogenie
    (study of the evolution of races)

16. **a.** dillatation   **b.** dilitation   **c.** dilatation   **d.** dillitation
    (widening)

17. **a.** garret   **b.** garrette   **c.** garette   **d.** garrett
    (room just beneath the roof)

18. **a.** collephon   **b.** colophon   **c.** colephon   **d.** coliphon
    (printer's inscription or emblem in a book)

19. **a.** tomaine   **b.** ptomaine   **c.** ptomain   **d.** phtomaine
    (food poisoning)

20. **a.** trekkor   **b.** treckor   **c.** treker   **d.** trekker
    (one who makes a difficult journey)

❃ No, No, No—Yes! 3

The three spellings shown for each word below are incorrect.
   Write in the correct spelling.

1. Beelzebubb   Beelzebbub   Bielzebub

   _____

2. misteltoe   mistletow   mis'letoe

   _____

3. gouwache   gouasche   g'washe

   _____

4. propedeutic   propideutic   propodeutic

   _____

5. murrh   murrhe   myrre

   _____

6. chickel   chikle   chickle

7. schrapnel   shrapnell   schrapnell

8. marriachi   mariacci   mariache

9. adscetitious   adcititious   adsititious

10. plankten   planckton   planckten

11. cemateries   cemetaries   cemmeteries

12. quintquennium   quinquenium   quinnquennium

13. empirean   empyrian   empiraen

14. piccador   picadore   piccadore

15. antenomasia   antinomasia   antonymasia

16. Sysiphian   Sisyphian   Sisiphean

17.	susurus	sussurus	sussurrus
18.	labbinotation	labynotation	labbanotation
19.	kich	kitch	kittch
20.	stevadore	stevidor	stevador
21.	spermiceti	spermecetti	spermicetti
22.	amarillus	ammarylus	amarylis
23.	dihptheria	diptheria	dyptheria
24.	antehistamine	antihistimine	antehistimine
25.	gryote	gruyot	griote

> *The late Miles Hanley, checking early New England letters and town records, noticed more than fifty spellings for forms of* receive, *including* receyve, resaived, recued, recieveing, *and* receaued.
>
> —Charlton Laird

✿ Five-Word Quizzicles 25–27

The words in each of these wee bees have not been idly chosen.
Write in the correct spelling.

Twenty-five

1. pas-TEESH _____
   (stylistic imitation or eclectic artistic composition)

2. PAST-ees _____
   (small meat pies)

3. puh-TIS-uh-ree _____
   (French pastry shop)

4. PAYS-lees _____
   (fabrics with a pattern of small curved figures)

5. pas-TEES _____
   (French anise-flavored liqueur)

---

*Spelling became not merely the shibboleth that distinguished one as a gent,
or even a lady. A century later bad spelling could ruin one's career as well as
one's social standing. Dr. Morell, a famous Inspector of Schools in England,
was quoted in 1877 as remarking that: "out of 1,972 failures in the Civil
Service examinations, 1,866 candidates were plucked for spelling. That is,
eighteen out of every nineteen who failed, failed in spelling.*

—Philip Howard

Twenty-six

1. SY-kluh-men _____
   (plant of the primrose family with nodding flowers of various colors)

2. SIK-uh-funt _____
   (servile but self-seeking follower or flatterer)

3. SY-uh-liz-um _____
   (superficial knowledge)

4. SY-dul _____
   (large beer glass or mug)

5. ZY-duh-ko _____
   (Southern Louisiana music featuring guitar, accordion, and washboard)

Twenty-seven

1. KAHL-por-ter _____
   (peddler of religious tracts or books)

2. SAWL-ter _____
   (book of biblical Psalms)

3. KLANG-er _____
   (loud ringing or clamorous noise)

4. OR-jer _____
   (excrement or manure)

5. lahn-GOR _____
   (long-tailed monkey of Asia)

❀ Say It and Spell It 10

Write in the correct spelling.

1. JIB-it _____
   (gallows)

2. TRY-er _____
   (one who tries)

3. TOOL _____
   (sheer fabric used for veils)

4. muh-RAH-kuh _____
   (shaken handheld rattle-sounding percussion instrument)

5. ser-VAYL _____
   (to watch clandestinely)

6. par-ox-IZ-mul _____
   (pertaining to a sudden seizure, attack, outburst, etc.)

7. MAT-ruh-lin-ee _____
   (familial descent through the maternal line)

8. ER-vruh _____
   (lifework of an artist, writer, or composer)

9. PEEK-ud _____
   (pale and sickly in appearance)

10. PLAT-un _____
    (roller on a typewriter or printer)

11. DOW-tee   _____

    (resolute or valiant)

12. eks-PAY-tree-uh-tiz-um   _____

    (residing outside one's native country)

13. AN-tik-lee   _____

    (merrily or clownishly)

14. troo-SO   _____

    (bride's personal belongings)

15. AIR-uh-fy   _____

    (to aerate)

16. GAL-uh-ses   _____

    (men's suspenders)

17. pap-uh-TREE   _____

    (fancy stationery)

18. uh-sof-uh-JEE-ul   _____

    (pertaining to the tube between the pharynx and the stomach)

19. les-ay-FAYR-iz-um   _____

    (economic belief in minimal governmental intervention)

20. HOOT-nan-ee   _____

    (informal folksinging session or concert)

❄ Fluster Cluster 2

Circle the misspelled words.

The impuned, rheumy-eyed Walloon picaroon was marooned—so far from Khartum—with some nasty baboons on a piccayune island beset with thick brume, coastal spume, and the heat of the simoom. But he found shelter at an old barracoon, littered with a broken-down brougham, rusty spittoons, and old insect cocoons, and nibbled on legumes and rather jujune macaroons.

❄ Three-Word Quizzicles 66–70

The words in each of these wee bees have not been idly chosen.
 Write in the correct spelling.

Sixty-six

1. hip-uh-PAHT-uh-mus   _____

   (large, rotund, hairless African river animal with short legs and a massive head)

2. soo-DAHN-uh-mus   _____

   (having or using a fictitious name)

3. KAL-us   _____

   (thickened area of skin)

Sixty-seven

1. HOOR-hownd   _____

   (bitter herb extract sometimes used in coughdrops)

2. HORN-blend   _____

   (mineral green to black in color)

3. HIP-noyd   _____

   (pertaining to sleep or hypnosis)

Sixty-eight

1. doo-uh-DEE-num   _____

   (part of the small intestine, from the stomach to the jejunum)

2. muh-LIB-duh-num   _____

   (silvery metallic element used in strengthening steel)

3. PAR-uh-nim   _____

   (word having the same root as another)

Sixty-nine

1. MA-duh-len   _____

   (small sweet shell-shaped cake)

2. MAH-diz-um   _____

   (belief in the awaited Muslim messiah)

3. mad-ri-LEN   _____

   (tomato-flavored consommé)

Seventy

1. ba-luh-KLAH-vuh _____

   (helmetlike wool cap for the face, neck, and shoulders)

2. BAH-kluh-va _____

   (honeyed thin-layered Turkish pastry with nuts)

3. LAHT-kuh _____

   (potato pancake)

❀ -Os or -Oes

Complete the correct plural spelling by filling in the space with *o* or *oe*.

1. kimon _____ s
2. fung _____ s
3. gring _____ s
4. fandang _____ s
5. ling _____ s
6. jing _____ s
7. her _____ s
8. farrag _____ s
9. caballer _____ s

10. fats _____ s
11. majordom _____ s
12. boler _____ s
13. curi _____ s
14. albin _____ s
15. sopran _____ s
16. vet _____ s
17. pistachi _____ s
18. potat _____ s

19. tomat _____ s
20. embry _____ s
21. seragli _____ s
22. fiasc _____ s
23. bass _____ s
24. hidalg _____ s
25. boz _____ s

❇ Multiple Choice 11

Circle the correct spelling.

1. **a.** pommagranate   **b.** pomagranite   c. pommegranate   d. pomegranate
   (large reddish fruit having many seeds)

2. **a.** nimiety   **b.** nemiety   c. nimmiety   d. numiety
   (excess)

3. **a.** descenary   **b.** decenary   c. decennery   d. decennary
   (period of ten years)

4. **a.** brusquerie   **b.** brusquery   c. bruskery   d. brusquerrie
   (bluntness or abruptness in manner)

5. **a.** bitummenous   **b.** bytumenous   c. bitumenous   d. bituminous
   (pertaining to soft coal)

6. **a.** anuroid   **b.** aneroid   c. anaroid   d. annaroid
   (using no liquid)

7. **a.** rehntgen   **b.** roentgen   c. rentgen   d. roentgon
   (unit of radiation)

8. **a.** Armmagedon   **b.** Armageddon   c. Armagedon   d. Armaggedon
   (final battle between good and evil)

9. **a.** parillogism   **b.** parallogism   c. paralogism   d. parilogism
   (logically false argument)

10. **a.** velleity   **b.** veliety   c. veleity   d. velliety
    (slight wish)

11. **a.** cautchuc   **b.** couchouc   **c.** caoutchouc   **d.** coutchouc
    (rubber)

12. **a.** monodnok   **b.** monodnoc   **c.** monadnock   **d.** monadnoc
    (isolated hill or mountain of rock)

13. **a.** vermeill   **b.** vermiell   **c.** vermiel   **d.** vermeil
    (gilded silver)

14. **a.** pharoah   **b.** pharoh   **c.** pharaoh   **d.** phaeraoh
    (ancient Egyptian ruler)

15. **a.** veruccose   **b.** verucose   **c.** verrucose   **d.** verruccose
    (warty)

16. **a.** berry-berry   **b.** berriberri   **c.** beriberi   **d.** buri-buri
    (disease caused by thiamine deficiency)

17. **a.** florescent   **b.** fleurescent   **c.** flourescent   **d.** fluorescent
    (absorbing and emitting radiation or light)

18. **a.** rhadamanthine   **b.** rhadimanthine   **c.** radhamanthine   **d.** radamanthine
    (strict but just)

19. **a.** nickolic   **b.** nicolic   **c.** niccollic   **d.** niccolic
    (containing nickel)

20. **a.** shekkel   **b.** shekell   **c.** shekel   **d.** schekel
    (Israeli coin)

❀ Five-Word Quizzicles 28–30

The words in each of these wee bees have not been idly chosen.
Write in the correct spelling.

Twenty-eight

1. dis-EV-er   _____

   (to separate)

2. dis-SIM-uh-tree   _____

   (lack of symmetry)

3. dis-RITH-me-uh   _____

   (recorded disturbance of brain waves rhythm)

4. dis-id-er-AH-tum   _____

   (something desired or needed)

5. dis-PEP-shuh   _____

   (indigestion)

One broad problem was never solved, and it has plagued English spelling to this day. The Greeks had supplied too few vowels, and nobody with power enough tried to overhaul the vowels in the Western vernacular. Scribes made some attempts (apparently they understood the desirability of letters representing sounds), but they had troubles. English was much fractured by dialect, and the transcribing was further confused by Norman copyists trying to write it with alphabetic traditions that had grown in Continental languages.

—Charlton Laird

Twenty-nine

1. HUM-uk   _____

   (knoll or small hill)

2. TIL-uk   _____

   (colored paste or powder spot worn on the forehead by Hindus)

3. DIB-uk   _____

   (in Jewish folklore, an indwelling wandering soul or demon)

4. SAF-ik   _____

   (lesbian)

5. TAR-mak   _____

   (road, runway, etc., paved with a mixture of crushed stones, tar, and bitumen)

Thirty

1. uh-mon-til-AH-do   _____

   (type of pale dry Spanish sherry)

2. maht-suh-REL-uh   _____

   (mild and moist white Italian cheese)

3. PUL-yuh-layt   _____

   (to germinate, breed, or teem)

4. bal-BRIG-un   _____

   (knitted cotton underwear fabric)

5. kam-uh-RIL-uh   _____

   (group of unofficial and secretive advisers)

❊ Classic Confusers

Some common but devil-to-spell words could be called classics.

Most of these twenty words—presented in the form of badly misspelled approximations—have laid low even highly educated people (as reported, among other places, in *Esquire* magazine years ago). They're misspelled so often that in some cases—to the chagrin of many language purists—dictionaries have thrown in the towel and now list the typical misspelled version as a permissible variant.

No thrown towels here, and we provide no definitions.

From these misspelled versions, you should be able to see (or silently hear) what word is meant in each case. Write in that word, correctly spelled. No alternative or variant spellings allowed.

1. uhnoynt _____
2. inokyewlate _____
3. desukayt _____
4. konkometent _____
5. assunine _____
6. ekstusee _____
7. ideeosinkrussy _____
8. rukoko _____
9. miniskyewl _____
10. mockusin _____

11. peeyewtrupheye _____
12. dilitont _____
13. kunsensis _____
14. leeayzon _____
15. puvillyun _____
16. sackrulijus _____
17. souperseed _____
18. impruhsareeo _____
19. oblugahto _____
20. dee rigoor _____

❄ Say It and Spell It 11

Write in the correct spelling.

1. **WEE-est**

   (most diminutive)

   _____

2. **PRO-tee-un**

   (able to change form, roles, etc., or show many faces)

   _____

3. **RIK-uts**

   (disease affecting bones in young people)

   _____

4. **RIK-uh-tee-nes**

   (shakiness or instability)

   _____

5. **mis-sej-uh-NAY-shun**

   (interracial mixing, especially sexual)

   _____

6. **SIB-ul**

   (female prophet of the ancient world)

   _____

7. **per-SPYR-ee**

   (sweaty)

   _____

8. **JUJ-ship**

   (office of a judge)

   _____

9. **juj-MAT-ik**

   (judicious)

   _____

10. **an-DROJ-uh-nee**

    (having both male and female characteristics)

    _____

11. vuh-ZEER

    (high official in the Ottoman Empire)

12. FYOO-suh-lahj

    (main body of an airplane)

13. KOZ-un

    (to persuade deceitfully or trick)

14. juh-LAT-in-us

    (like jelly)

15. SHOO-in

    (sure and unquestionably expected winner)

16. KAT-uh-muh-ran

    (double-hulled boat)

17. fan-far-uh-NAYD

    (grand boasting or bluster)

18. AW-tahr-kee

    (national economic self-sufficiency)

19. MAN-uh-kuls

    (handcuffs)

20. for-or-DAYN

    (determine ahead of time or predestine)

❃ Three-Word Quizzicles 71–75

The words in each of these wee bees have not been idly chosen.
Write in the correct spelling.

Seventy-one

1. PER-lyoo   _____

   (outlying or peripheral area)

2. VIN-duh-loo   _____

   (dish of India that blends various spices)

3. KEE-poo   _____

   (Incan calculating device of knotted cords of different colors)

Seventy-two

1. KLAV-uh-kord   _____

   (early, soft-sounding stringed keyboard instrument)

2. AW-toh-klayv   _____

   (pressurized steam-heated apparatus for sterilizing medical instruments)

3. KLA-vi-kul   _____

   (collarbone)

If a kid says, "Dad, how do you spell fisickle?" and Dad, hoping to teach self-reliance as well as spelling, says, "Look it up," he'll just be jamming a larger wedge into the generation gap.

—Thomas Middleton

Seventy-three

1. IM-uh-nent
   _____

   (inherent, within, or indwelling)

2. uh-MOL-yent
   _____

   (something that softens or soothes)

3. uh-MOL-yuh-ment
   _____

   (financial rewards, compensation, or perquisite)

Seventy-four

1. DIN-jee-nes
   _____

   (oppressively shabby, dirty, or lightless state or condition)

2. DEN-gay
   _____

   (infectious, fevered disease transmitted by mosquitoes)

3. DING-ees
   _____

   (ships' small boats, lifeboats, or tenders)

Seventy-five

1. AR-muh-ler-ee (~ sphere)
   _____

   (old astronomical apparatus with angled rings for the celestial equator, ecliptic, etc.)

2. EM-uh-ser-ee
   _____

   (agent or representative sent on a mission)

3. LAH-muh-ser-ee
   _____

   (monastery of Buddhist monks)

❋ -Er or -Or 1

Complete the correct spelling by filling in the space with *er* or *or*.

1. estimat ____
2. facilitat ____
3. hallucinat ____
4. mutilat ____
5. repudiat ____
6. infect ____
7. separat ____
8. discriminat ____
9. forfeit ____
10. extirpat ____
11. depredat ____
12. placat ____
13. inculcat ____
14. insinuat ____
15. predict ____
16. perpetuat ____
17. enumerat ____
18. cultivat ____
19. accumulat ____
20. pollinat ____
21. educat ____
22. consummat ____
23. proselytiz ____
24. improvisat ____
25. arbit ____

❋ Multiple Choice 12

Circle the correct spelling.

1. **a.** hazenpfeffer **b.** hasenpfeffer **c.** hazenfeffer **d.** hatzenpfeffer
   (rabbit stew)

2. **a.** loup **b.** loupe **c.** louppe **d.** loope
   (jeweler's magnifying glass)

3. **a.** kiosk **b.** quiosque **c.** kyosque **d.** keyosk
   (newsstand structure)

4. **a.** pallette **b.** palette **c.** pallet **d.** pallett
   (painter's handheld pigment board)

5. **a.** cocquettry   **b.** coquetry   **c.** coquetterie   **d.** coquettry
   (flirtatiousness)

6. **a.** inards   **b.** innerds   **c.** innards   **d.** innerdes
   (animal's internal parts)

7. **a.** opalesent   **b.** opalescent   **c.** opallescent   **d.** opellescent
   (reflecting light iridescently)

8. **a.** sarsparella   **b.** sarsaparilla   **c.** sasparella   **d.** sassaparilla
   (flavorful root used in a soft drink)

9. **a.** buccanneer   **b.** buckaneer   **c.** bucanneer   **d.** buccaneer
   (freebooter or pirate)

10. **a.** naperie   **b.** napery   **c.** napperie   **d.** nappery
    (table linen)

11. **a.** paragoric   **b.** paregoric   **c.** parigoric   **d.** parragoric
    (pain-relieving camphorated tincture of opium)

12. **a.** aperitif   **b.** aper'tif   **c.** appertif   **d.** apperitif
    (premeal cocktail)

13. **a.** compasse mentice   **b.** compus mentis   **c.** compass mentis   **d.** compos mentis
    (sound of mind)

14. **a.** revellie   **b.** reveille   **c.** revvely   **d.** revveille
    (military wake-up call)

15. **a.** schnaps   **b.** shnapps   **c.** schnapps   **d.** shnaps
    (strong Dutch gin)

16. **a.** psychodelic   **b.** psychedelic   **c.** psychadelic   **d.** psychadellic
    (pertaining to an altered state of perception, awareness, etc.; hallucinatory)

17. **a.** eleemosynery   **b.** eleymosynary   **c.** eleymosinary   **d.** eleemosynary
   (charitable)

18. **a.** Chris Cringle   **b.** Kris Kringle   **c.** Kriss Kringle   **d.** Chriss Kringle
   (Santa Claus)

19. **a.** hermineutics   **b.** hermaneutics   **c.** hermeneutics   **d.** hermanutics
   (scholarly interpretation as a method, especially of Scripture)

20. **a.** piranha   **b.** pirannah   **c.** piranna   **d.** piranah
   (carnivorous South American fish)

❊ Five-Word Quizzicles 31–33

The words in each of these wee bees have not been idly chosen.
   Write in the correct spelling.

Thirty-one

1. **POL-up** _____
   (growth or tumor, usually not malignant, of a mucus membrane)

2. **DOL-up** _____
   (lump or portion spooned out)

3. **JOO-lip** _____
   (sweet and syrupy drink, as one with liquor, sugar, mint, and crushed ice)

4. **TIT-up** _____
   (to prance or move in a lively way)

5. **TER-nup** _____
   (plant of the mustard family whose root is an edible vegetable)

Thirty-two

1. too-PAY   _____

   (hairpiece for a bald head or bald spot)

2. toh-PEE   _____

   (light helmetlike sun hat of pith)

3. TOPE   _____

   (brownish gray)

4. TOH-pee   _____

   (African antelope, the sassaby)

5. TOH-pee-er-ee   _____

   (garden of artfully trimmed, often animal-shaped trees or shrubs)

Thirty-three

1. fil-uh-PEENZ   _____

   (country and archipelago of East Asia)

2. fil-uh-PEE-no   _____

   (native or citizen of the above republic)

3. FIL-ips screwdriver   _____

   (tool for use with screws having a cross-shaped slot)

4. fil-LIP-ik   _____

   (bitterly harsh declamatory tirade)

5. fil-ee-o-py-uh-TIS-tik   _____

   (pertaining to cultural veneration of ancestors, forebears, or tradition)

❊ Spell for Your Supper

Here is the dinner menu from the Hungry Bee Café. However, before you can order, you must find the seventeen misspellings.

1. lilikoi
2. blanc mangé
3. jumbalaya
4. fettucelle
5. baba au rhum
6. Gewürztraminer
7. turmeric
8. bagette
9. chimichanga
10. Valpolacella
11. picadillo
12. beignets au fromage
13. ratatouille
14. raclette
15. beef bourgingnon
16. Nesslerode pie
17. calamari
18. perciatelli
19. wasabe
20. Chilaen sea bass
21. langostine
22. ugli fruit
23. potatoes rissolées
24. quesadilla
25. yakitori
26. gallantine of turkey
27. tortellini
28. avgolemono
29. loukanika
30. anatto
31. Verdicchio
32. Mornay sauce
33. gaspergou
34. flageolets
35. rémoulade
36. kreplack
37. cannalone
38. café brûlot
39. saltimbocca
40. feijoada
41. Béchamel sauce
42. lebkuchen
43. béarnaise sauce
44. Poiley-Fuissé
45. radicchio
46. kumquat
47. arrugula
48. pappadam
49. anasazzi beans
50. finocchio

> So long as the effective use of language is a matter of memorising and applying rules, there is no scope for the outstanding achievement that demands outstanding effort. We do not congratulate a man on the excellence of his spelling.
>
> —G. L. Brook

❊ Three-Word Quizzicles 76–80

The words in each of these wee bees have not been idly chosen.
Write in the correct spelling.

Seventy-six

1. PY-see-un   _____

   (in astrology, pertaining to the twelfth sign of the zodiac)

2. EP-uh-seen   _____

   (having characteristics of the opposite sex)

3. PY-seen   _____

   (pertaining to fish)

Seventy-seven

1. sit-ruh-NEL-uh   _____

   (aromatic oil used in perfumes and insect repellent)

2. uh-MIG-duh-luh   _____

   (almond-shaped gray matter in the brain's temporal lobe)

3. moo-LAY-tuh   _____

   (in bullfighting, red cloth used climactically by the matador)

One of the easy cases is that of the boy who said, "I can spell banana all right, only I don't know when to stop."

—Edna L. Furness

Seventy-eight

1. FYOO-shuh
   (shrub with nodding purple or red flowers)

2. fuh-KAH-shuh
   (seasoned flat Italian bread)

3. NAF-thuh
   (liquid hydrocarbon mixture used in solvents)

Seventy-nine

1. FAL-un-ster-ee
   (cooperative community of followers of social reformer Charles Fourier)

2. FAY-shee-eez
   (medically, general appearance of one's face in terms of disease symptoms)

3. fuh-LAN-jees
   (in anatomy, finger or toe bones)

Eighty

1. LAHR-berd
   (on a ship's port side)

2. BLAG-erd
   (scoundrel)

3. HAL-berd
   (fifteenth- to sixteenth-century weapon, a long shaft with battle-ax and spike)

✵ Say It and Spell It 12

Write in the correct spelling.

1. MO-zee
   (stroll idly or saunter)

   _____

2. PO-zee
   (bouquet)

   _____

3. ham-uh-DRY-ud
   (wood nymph)

   _____

4. SIB-uh-ry-tiz-um
   (indulgence in luxury and sensuality)

   _____

5. kon-san-GWIN-ee-us
   (of the same bloodline or ancestry)

   _____

6. BRIT-un
   (native of Great Britain)

   _____

7. CLEE-kee
   (narrowly or pettily exclusive socially)

   _____

8. RID-duns
   (success in being free of)

   _____

9. im-BROHL-yo
   (unwanted confused encounter or situation)

   _____

10. SPY-nee-nes
    (having pointed or sharp protrusions)

    _____

11. bahm-ber-DEER

   (aircraft crew member)

   _____

12. YES-es

   (affirmations)

   _____

13. ETH-uh-nawl

   (colorless liquid used in certain fuels)

   _____

14. MER-muh-rer

   (one speaking softly or indistinctly)

   _____

15. sez-YUR-uh

   (pause or interruption)

   _____

16. HEN-er-ee

   (poultry farm)

   _____

17. RIV-uh-ter

   (person or thing that commands attention)

   _____

18. SHEEK-lee

   (in an elegantly stylish way)

   _____

19. sil-AN-tro

   (flavorful coriander leaves)

   _____

20. BUL-yahn

   (clear, often beef- or chicken-flavored soup)

   _____

❊ -Er or -Or 2

Complete the correct spelling by filling in the space with *er* or *or*.

1. abbreviat _____
2. confiscat _____
3. sojourn _____
4. formulat _____
5. masticat _____
6. subjugat _____
7. obliterat _____
8. dissertat _____
9. abscond _____

10. punctuat _____
11. initiat _____
12. contest _____
13. tergiversat _____
14. execrat _____
15. perpetrat _____
16. inveigh _____
17. advocat _____
18. disburs _____

19. illuminat _____
20. extrapolat _____
21. attract _____
22. pontificat _____
23. alienat _____
24. denigrat _____
25. dissimulat _____

❊ Multiple Choice 13

Circle the correct spelling.

1. **a.** sennery   **b.** senary   **c.** sennary   **d.** sennory
   (pertaining to the number six or having six parts)

2. **a.** ophthalmology   **b.** ohpthalmology   **c.** opthalmology   **d.** oppthalmology
   (medical field pertaining to the eyes)

3. **a.** bouillibaisse   **b.** bouillabaisse   **c.** bouillebaisse   **d.** bouillabaise
   (fish stew)

4. **a.** caduceous   **b.** caduceus   **c.** cadutious   **d.** caducious
   (symbol of entwined snakes on a staff; physician's symbol)

5. **a.** Shaeol   **b.** Sheol   **c.** Sheole   **d.** Sheoll
   (*Hebrews' realm of the dead*)

6. **a.** camillia   **b.** chamelia   **c.** camellia   **d.** chamellia
   (*ornamental shrub with roselike flowers*)

7. **a.** sibilant   **b.** sibillant   **c.** syballant   **d.** sybillant
   (*making an s or sh sound*)

8. **a.** smorrgasbord   **b.** smorgasboard   **c.** smorgesboard   **d.** smorgasbord
   (*buffet meal*)

9. **a.** cameraderie   **b.** camaradery   **c.** camaraderie   **d.** cameradery
   (*comradeship*)

10. **a.** jittney   **b.** jitney   **c.** gitney   **d.** djittney
    (*small bus*)

11. **a.** appoggiatura   **b.** appogiatura   **c.** apogiatura   **d.** apoggiatura
    (*in music, an embellishing note*)

12. **a.** maggety   **b.** maggoty   **c.** maggotty   **d.** magitty
    (*infested with legless grubs*)

13. **a.** chuka   **b.** chukah   **c.** chukkah   **d.** chukka
    (*ankle-high boot*)

14. **a.** apurtenance   **b.** appertenence   **c.** appurtenence   **d.** appurtenance
    (*subordinate part*)

15. **a.** chapleted   **b.** chapletted   **c.** chappletted   **d.** chappleted
    (*wearing a head wreath*)

16. **a.** zeppillin   **b.** zeppolinn   **c.** zepellin   **d.** zeppelin
    (football-shaped airship)

17. **a.** soutain   **b.** sutayne   **c.** soutane   **d.** soutaine
    (cleric's cassock)

18. **a.** tohubohu   **b.** tohoubohue   **c.** tohoobohoo   **d.** tohuebohue
    (disaster or chaos)

19. **a.** cirhosis   **b.** cirhossis   **c.** cirrhosis   **d.** scirhossis
    (liver disease)

20. **a.** scimter   **b.** scimitar   **c.** scimater   **d.** scimatar
    (curved saber of the historical Middle East)

❊ Three-Word Quizzicles 81–85

The words in each of these wee bees have not been idly chosen.
Write in the correct spelling.

Eighty-one

1. BRAK-un   _____
   (thicket or area overgrown with a weedy fern)

2. KROK-un   _____
   (in legend, a Scandinavian sea monster)

3. LYK-un   _____
   (plantlike organism, a fungus that grows symbiotically with algae)

Eighty-two

1. TAM-bur   _____

   (distinctive quality of tone or voice, apart from pitch or loudness)

2. TEM-bler   _____

   (earthquake)

3. TUM-ler   _____

   (entertaining social director, host, MC, etc., at a Jewish resort)

Eighty-three

1. SIR-inks   _____

   (vocal organ in birds)

2. suh-ROO-mun   _____

   (earwax)

3. sy-REE-nee-un   _____

   (pertaining to aquatic herbivorous mammals such as the manatee)

Eighty-four

1. AT-ohl   _____

   (ringlike coral island enclosing a lagoon)

2. AV-uh-tar   _____

   (incarnation, personification, or embodiment)

3. AT-er   _____

   (fragrant essential oil from flowers)

Eighty-five

1. **BAR-bit** _____

   (tropical toucan-related bird with a broad bill and colorful plumage)

2. **bar-BET** _____

   (protective cylinder around a warship's gun turret)

3. **BUR-but** _____

   (freshwater fish resembling the cod)

❊ American Cities

Circle the correct spelling.

1. **a.** Talahasee   **b.** Tallahassie   **c.** Tallihassie   **d.** Tallahassee
   (Florida)

2. **a.** Albaquerque   **b.** Albuqerque   **c.** Albuquerque   **d.** Albequerque
   (New Mexico)

3. **a.** Ypsalanti   **b.** Ypsilante   **c.** Ypsilanti   **d.** Ypselanti
   (Michigan)

4. **a.** Wapiton   **b.** Wahpiton   **c.** Wapeton   **d.** Wahpeton
   (North Dakota)

5. **a.** Corvalis   **b.** Corvalliss   **c.** Corvallas   **d.** Corvallis
   (Oregon)

6. **a.** Oskallousa   **b.** Oskaloosa   **c.** Oscilloosa   **d.** Oskilloosa
   (Iowa)

7. **a.** Chattennouga   **b.** Chattanooga   **c.** Chattinooga   **d.** Chattannooga
   (*Tennessee*)

8. **a.** Schenechtedy   **b.** Schenectedy   **c.** Schenechtady   **d.** Schenectady
   (*New York*)

9. **a.** Wilkes-Bare   **b.** Wilkes-Barre   **c.** Wilkes-Barrie   **d.** Wilks-Barre
   (*Pennsylvania*)

10. **a.** Chillicoth   **b.** Chilicothe   **c.** Chillecothe   **d.** Chillicothe
    (*Ohio*)

11. **a.** Ammarilo   **b.** Ammarrilo   **c.** Amarillo   **d.** Amarrillo
    (*Texas*)

12. **a.** Champaign   **b.** Champain   **c.** Champagne   **d.** Champaigne
    (*Illinois*)

13. **a.** Boguloosa   **b.** Bogaloosa   **c.** Bogalusa   **d.** Bogulusa
    (*Louisiana*)

14. **a.** Casper   **b.** Caspor   **c.** Caspur   **d.** Caspere
    (*Wyoming*)

15. **a.** Manasquan   **b.** Mannasquan   **c.** Manasquon   **d.** Mannisquan
    (*New Jersey*)

16. **a.** Elkharte   **b.** Elkheart   **c.** Elkhart   **d.** Elkhard
    (*Indiana*)

17. **a.** Meriden   **b.** Meridan   **c.** Merriden   **d.** Merridan
    (*Connecticut*)

18. **a.** Fredericksburg   **b.** Fredericsburg   **c.** Fredericsberg   **d.** Fredericksberg
(Virginia)

19. **a.** Montpellier   **b.** Montpellior   **c.** Montpelier   **d.** Montpelior
(Vermont)

20. **a.** Savanna   **b.** Savvannah   **c.** Savanah   **d.** Savannah
(Georgia)

21. **a.** Scheboygun   **b.** Scheboygan   **c.** Sheboygun   **d.** Sheboygan
(Wisconsin)

22. **a.** Misoulla   **b.** Missula   **c.** Missoulla   **d.** Missoula
(Montana)

23. **a.** Parigould   **b.** Parragould   **c.** Paragould   **d.** Parrigould
(Arkansas)

24. **a.** Tuskaloosa   **b.** Tuscaloosa   **c.** Tuskeloosa   **d.** Tuscalloosa
(Alabama)

25. **a.** Brainerd   **b.** Brainerde   **c.** Brainard   **d.** Brainarde
(Minnesota)

26. **a.** Atcheson   **b.** Atchison   **c.** Atchesson   **d.** Atchisson
(Kansas)

27. **a.** McAllister   **b.** McAlester   **c.** McAllester   **d.** MacAlister
(Oklahoma)

28. **a.** Toule   **b.** Toole   **c.** Toulle   **d.** Tooele
(Utah)

29. **a**. Petaluma **b**. Pettaluma **c**. Petiluma **d**. Petalluma
    (California)

30. **a**. Pocatelo **b**. Pocotelo **c**. Pocotello **d**. Pocatello
    (Idaho)

31. **a**. Spartenberg **b**. Spartanberg **c**. Spartenburg **d**. Spartanburg
    (South Carolina)

32. **a**. Paducah **b**. Paduccah **c**. Padducah **d**. Padukah
    (Kentucky)

33. **a**. Vermilion **b**. Vermileon **c**. Vermillion **d**. Vermilleon
    (South Dakota)

34. **a**. Woonsocket **b**. Woonsokette **c**. Woonsockett **d**. Woonsockette
    (Rhode Island)

35. **a**. Buckhannon **b**. Buckhanan **c**. Buckhanon **d**. Buckhannan
    (West Virginia)

36. **a**. Chickopie **b**. Chickopee **c**. Chicopie **d**. Chicopee
    (Massachusetts)

37. **a**. Winachee **b**. Winache **c**. Wenache **d**. Wenatchee
    (Washington)

38. **a**. Kechikan **b**. Ketchikan **c**. Kechekan **d**. Ketchekan
    (Alaska)

39. **a**. Wiluku **b**. Waillukoo **c**. Wailluku **d**. Wailuku
    (Hawaii)

40. **a.** Hattiesburg **b.** Hattysburg **c.** Hatteesburg **d.** Hattiesberg
(Mississippi)

41. **a.** Walsenburg **b.** Wallsenburg **c.** Walsinburg **d.** Walsunburg
(Colorado)

42. **a.** Plastow **b.** Plaisto **c.** Plaistow **d.** Playsto
(New Hampshire)

43. **a.** Millinockit **b.** Millinockett **c.** Millinockitt **d.** Millinocket
(Maine)

44. **a.** Sedalia **b.** Sidalia **c.** Sedallia **d.** Sidallia
(Missouri)

45. **a.** Winnimuca **b.** Winnemucca **c.** Winnemuca **d.** Winnimucca
(Nevada)

46. **a.** Dundalk **b.** Dundalke **c.** Dundolk **d.** Dundaulk
(Maryland)

47. **a.** Smyrrna **b.** Smyrna **c.** Smyrnna **d.** Smirnna
(Delaware)

48. **a.** Canapolis **b.** Kanapolis **c.** Cannapolis **d.** Kannapolis
(North Carolina)

49. **a.** Holldridge **b.** Holdridge **c.** Holdrege **d.** Holdrige
(Nebraska)

50. **a.** Bisby **b.** Bisbe **c.** Bisbee **d.** Bisbie
(Arizona)

✿ Say It and Spell It 13

Write in the correct spelling.

1. **SHMOZE** _____
   (jerks or losers)

2. **PWER-uh-lee** _____
   (childishly or immaturely)

3. **mal-uh-GAYN-yuh** _____
   (Spanish dance similar to a fandango)

4. **kon-tuh-MEEL-yus** _____
   (contemptuously insulting or abusing)

5. **re-MIT-unce** _____
   (transmittal of money)

6. **re-MIT-unt** _____
   (alternating in prevalence or severity of symptoms)

7. **AP-uh-them** _____
   (pithy saying)

8. **PUN-chun** _____
   (pointed piercing or stamping tool)

9. **KROOP** _____
   (throat condition caused by a hoarse or sharp cough)

10. **MY-ree** _____
    (characteristic of a mire)

11. JES-o _____

   (plaster of Paris whose surface is prepared for painting)

12. LIN-gun-ber-ee _____

   (fruit of the mountain cranberry)

13. NAYR-doo-wel _____

   (idler or good-for-nothing)

14. ay-byoo-PRO-fin _____

   (anti-inflammatory medication)

15. puh-RY-uh-tuls _____

   (college or campus living regulations)

16. PIK-nik _____

   (short and muscular in human body type)

17. HOY-dun _____

   (bold, spirited girl or tomboy)

18. fa-ruh-SAY-iz-um _____

   (unctuous hypocrisy)

19. PAK-ut _____

   (mail boat)

20. SOL-fa _____

   (conventional syllables used in singing tones of the scale)

❊ Five-Word Quizzicles 34–36

The words in each of these wee bees have not been idly chosen.
Write in the correct spelling.

Thirty-four

1. ri-SEN-shun   _____

   (critical textual revision)

2. ri-SIZH-un   _____

   (canceling, annuling, or voiding)

3. ri-SIS-uh-bul   _____

   (capable of being canceled, annulled, etc.)

4. ri-SID-uh-viz-um   _____

   (reverting to earlier tendencies, especially criminal behavior)

5. ri-SEE-duh   _____

   (grayish green or light olive)

> What most complicates the situation is that English spelling is haunted by
> what William Watt calls "the little ghosts of silent letters." Indeed, it has
> been estimated that two thirds of our lexicon is populated with these mischie-
> vous specters, leading Thorstein Veblen to proclaim: "English orthography
> satisfies all the requirements of the canons of reputability under the law of
> conspicuous waste."
>
> —Richard Lederer

Thirty-five

1. RY-thing   _____
   (*moving one's body in a tormented or twisted way*)

2. TY-thing   _____
   (*giving one tenth of one's income in support of a church, religion, etc.*)

3. LAY-thing   _____
   (*shaping wood, metal, etc., by using a machine that holds and rotates the piece*)

4. SEE-thing   _____
   (*in a state of simmering or volatile agitation, turmoil, anger, etc.*)

5. SY-thing   _____
   (*mowing grass with a long-handled tool having an angled curved blade*)

Thirty-six

1. KAHT-uh   _____
   (*waist-length surplice*)

2. kah-tuh-LEED-un   _____
   (*first leaf developed by a seed plant embryo*)

3. KAH-tah   _____
   (*set of martial arts positions and movements*)

4. kuh-DEEV   _____
   (*Turkish viceroy who formerly ruled Egypt*)

5. KAHM-boo   _____
   (*dried kelp seasoning used in Japanese cookery*)

❋ Field Test 1: Social Sciences

Terms from history, political science, psychology, anthropology, sociology . . .

Circle the correct spelling.

1. **a.** Australopithecine   **b.** Australepithecine   **c.** Australopithecene
    (pertaining to an extinct genus of bipedal hominids of one to four million years ago)

2. **a.** appotropaic   **b.** appotropaik   **c.** apotropaic
    (warding off evil superstitiously or through rituals, magic, etc.)

3. **a.** hennotheism   **b.** hennitheism   **c.** henotheism
    (belief in one god but allowing the possible existence of others)

4. **a.** sattiagraha   **b.** satyagraha   **c.** satiagraha
    (nonviolent or passive resistance as practiced by Mahatma Gandhi)

5. **a.** Peloponnesian War   **b.** Peloppenesian War   **c.** Peloppanesian War
    (fifth-century-BC conflict in Greece between Athens and Sparta)

6. **a.** Menshevik   **b.** Menchavik   **c.** Menschavik
    (in the Russian Revolution, one belonging to the faction opposing the Bolsheviks)

7. **a.** quadreumanous   **b.** quadrumanous   **c.** quadrumenous
    ("four-handed," like primates, who have opposable first digits)

8. **a.** dolikocephalic   **b.** dolichocephalic   **c.** dolechocephalic
    (in anthropological measurement, having a relatively long head)

9. **a.** postrimogeniture   **b.** postrhemogeniture   **c.** postremogeniture
    (system of inheritance whereby the deceased's estate goes to the youngest son)

10. **a.** annancastic   **b.** anankastic   **c.** anancastic

(having personality traits that are obsessive or compulsive)

11. **a.** suzerainty   **b.** suzeranty   **c.** suzerranty

(political dominion, as over a subject nation in international matters)

12. **a.** agiorniamento   **b.** aggiorniamento   **c.** aggiornamento

(modernizing process, as of a society, culture, institution, etc.)

13. **a.** Olduvai Gorge   **b.** Olldevai Gorge   **c.** Oldouvai Gorge

(Tanzania site of discovered Australopithecine fossils and paleolithic tools)

14. **a.** pottlatche   **b.** potlach   **c.** potlatch

(Northwestern Native American festival of lavish, competitive giving and sometimes destruction by the host of his own property)

15. **a.** Wexler-Belleview   **b.** Wechsler-Bellview   **c.** Wechsler-Bellevue

(intelligence scale used in psychological testing)

16. **a.** Thermopoli   **b.** Thermopouli   **c.** Thermopylae

(Greek pass where the Persians defeated Sparta in 480 BC)

17. **a.** Ashkenazim   **b.** Ashkanazim   **c.** Aschkanazim

(branch of Jewry, those from central and northern Europe and their descendants)

18. **a.** irredentism   **b.** iridentism   **c.** irridentism

(advocacy of repossession of neighboring territory that has historical, ethnic, etc., links with one's own country)

19. **a.** kakistocracy   **b.** cacistocracy   **c.** kakistokracy

(government by the worst people)

20. **a.** Asheoulian   **b.** Achieulean   **c.** Acheulean

(pertaining to a tool-culture stage that is part of the Lower Paleolithic Period)

21. **a**. cassus belli **b**. casus belli **c**. causus beli
    (event, action, etc., cited or used to justify waging war)

22. **a**. aidetic **b**. aidetik **c**. eidetic
    (highly vivid and detailed in one's recall of visual images)

23. **a**. hebyphrenia **b**. hebephrenia **c**. hebiphrenia
    (type of schizophrenia often developing during adolescence)

24. **a**. antekathecsis **b**. antikathexis **c**. anticathexis
    (in psychiatry, a shift from one emotion to its opposite)

25. **a**. Kemal Attaturque **b**. Kemal Ataturk **c**. Kemal Atteturke
    (military leader and founder of modern Turkey, 1881–1938)

26. **a**. ekistics **b**. eichistics **c**. echistiks
    (scientific study of human settlements, their design, planning, etc.)

27. **a**. Appommatax **b**. Apommatax **c**. Appomattax
    (Virginia site of Lee's surrender to Grant in 1865)

28. **a**. labret **b**. labarette **c**. labiarette
    (lip ornament)

29. **a**. fraterie **b**. phratry **c**. fratry
    (clan or other kinship intratribal grouping)

30. **a**. Stokhanovite **b**. Stachanovite **c**. Stakhanovite
    (exemplarily productive and honored Soviet worker)

❊ Three-Word Quizzicles 86–90

The words in each of these wee bees have not been idly chosen.
Write in the correct spelling.

Eighty-six

1. DY-ker

   _____

   (small African antelope with horns)

2. SY-pher

   _____

   (to overlap and even edges to form a flush surface)

3. FREE-ker

   _____

   (one who illegally gains technical access to the telephone system)

Eighty-seven

1. O-dee-um

   _____

   (building of ancient Greece for theater, music, and poetry)

2. O-dee-um

   _____

   (state of being the object of spite, blame, hatred, etc.)

3. o-BAHD

   _____

   (poem, song, etc., in tribute to the dawn)

It is a pity that Chawcer, who had geneyus, was so unedicated. He's the wuss speller I know of.

—Artemus Ward

Eighty-eight

1. PIL-yun

   (riding cushion or saddle for a woman)

2. MIN-yun

   (slavishly obedient follower or underling)

3. MIN-yun

   (in Jewish worship, quorum for a service)

Eighty-nine

1. guh-ZEL

   (small and swift African or Asian antelope)

2. gaz-uh-TEER

   (dictionary or index of geography)

3. laz-uh-RET-o

   (hospital, building, etc., for treatment of contagious diseases)

Ninety

1. uh-KRAHS-tik

   (verses in which the lines' first letters vertically form a word, message, etc.)

2. kat-uh-KRES-tik

   (using a wrong word or phrase or straining a figure of speech)

3. kat-uh-BAT-ik

   (pertaining to wind caused by cold air flowing down a slope)

❋ Multiple Choice 14

Circle the correct spelling.

1. **a.** jelignite **b.** gelignite **c.** gellignite **d.** jellignite
   (type of dynamite)

2. **a.** vacqueros **b.** vaqueroes **c.** vaqueros **d.** vacquéros
   (cowboys)

3. **a.** dacquerie **b.** daiquiri **c.** daiqueri **d.** daiquerie
   (rum and lime juice cocktail)

4. **a.** annemometer **b.** annemmometer **c.** animometer **d.** anemometer
   (instrument measuring wind force)

5. **a.** topsy-turviness **b.** topsi-turvyness **c.** topsi-turviness **d.** topsy-turvyness
   (upside-downness or confusion)

6. **a.** topsi-turvidom **b.** topsi-turvydom **c.** topsy-turvydom **d.** topsy-turvidom
   (upside-downness or confusion)

7. **a.** louaue **b.** luau **c.** luaue **d.** louau
   (Hawaiian banquet)

8. **a.** spinacker **b.** spinaker **c.** spinnackor **d.** spinnaker
   (large triangular sail)

9. **a.** dirndle **b.** derndl **c.** dirnndl **d.** dirndl
   (tight-bodiced peasant-style dress)

10. **a.** finagle **b.** phenagle **c.** phinagle **d.** finnagle
    (to scheme or acquire deviously)

11. **a**. turrete   **b**. terete   **c**. turete   **d**. territe
    (somewhat cylindrical but with tapered ends)

12. **a**. spiellunker   **b**. speelunker   **c**. spelelunker   **d**. spelunker
    (hobbyist cave explorer)

13. **a**. kindergardener   **b**. kindergartner   **c**. kindergardner   **d**. kindergardenner
    (pupil usually four to six years old)

14. **a**. jodhpurs   **b**. jodpurhs   **c**. johdpurs   **d**. jodphurs
    (riding breeches)

15. **a**. barret   **b**. barrette   **c**. barette   **d**. barrete
    (woman's hair clip)

16. **a**. mannicoti   **b**. mannicotte   **c**. manicotti   **d**. mannicotti
    (Italian pasta dish)

17. **a**. paene   **b**. paeane   **c**. peane   **d**. paean
    (tribute or hymn of praise)

18. **a**. slavies   **b**. slaveys   **c**. slavees   **d**. slavveys
    (female servants)

19. **a**. fricassee   **b**. friccisee   **c**. fricissee   **d**. friccasee
    (stewed chicken dish)

20. **a**. marquis   **b**. markee   **c**. markey   **d**. marquee
    (theater entrance canopy)

World Geography

Circle the correct spelling.

1. a. Lichtenstein | b. Liechtenstein | c. Leichtenstein
   (principality between Switzerland and Austria)

2. a. Adelaide | b. Addelaide | c. Adelade
   (Australian city)

3. a. Machue Pichu | b. Machu Picchu | c. Machu Pichu
   (ancient Inca ruins site near Cuzco, Peru)

4. a. Abu Dabbi | b. Abbu Dhabi | c. Abu Dhabi
   (United Arab Emirates sheikhdom)

5. a. Saskatchewan | b. Saskatchuan | c. Saskachewan
   (Canadian province)

6. a. Kouai | b. Kauai | c. Kauei
   (northwestern island of Hawaii)

7. a. Apennines | b. Appennines | c. Appenines
   (mountain system extending down peninsula of Italy)

8. a. Reyahd | b. Riyadh | c. Riadh
   (Saudi Arabian city)

9. a. Upsalla | b. Upssala | c. Uppsala
   (Swedish city)

10. a. Djebouti | b. Djibouti | c. Djibbouti
    (country of eastern Africa)

11. **a**. Tyrrenian Sea   **b**. Tyrhennian Sea   **c**. Tyrrhenian Sea
    (arm of the Mediterranean Sea west of Italy and north of Sicily)

12. **a**. Reykhjavik   **b**. Reykjavik   **c**. Rekjavik
    (Icelandic city)

13. **a**. Kyrhgsztan   **b**. Kyrgyzstan   **c**. Kyrggistan
    (country of west-central Asia)

14. **a**. Saulte Saint Marie   **b**. Sault Sainte Marie   **c**. Soulte Ste. Marie
    (Canadian city)

15. **a**. Hokeido   **b**. Hokkaido   **c**. Hokkeido
    (Japan's second largest island, north of Honshu)

16. **a**. Leistershire   **b**. Leicestershire   **c**. Liestershire
    (English county)

17. **a**. Marreceibo   **b**. Marracaibo   **c**. Maracaibo
    (Venezuelan city)

18. **a**. Kafekluben   **b**. Kaffeclubben   **c**. Kaffeeklubben
    (Arctic island near Greenland, northernmost point of land in the world)

19. **a**. Brahmiputra   **b**. Brahmaputra   **c**. Brahmahputra
    (Asian river)

20. **a**. Edinborough   **b**. Edinbrough   **c**. Edinburgh
    (Scottish city)

21. **a**. Ballaric Islands   **b**. Balaric Islands   **c**. Balearic Islands
    (Spanish islands in the Mediterranean)

22. **a.** Phnom Pen   **b.** Pnom Phen   **c.** Phnom Penh
    (Cambodian city)

23. **a.** Lake Tittikaka   **b.** Lake Titicaca   **c.** Lake Titikaka
    (lake at the boundary of Bolivia and Peru)

24. **a.** Johanesberg   **b.** Johannesburg   **c.** Johannesburgh
    (South African city)

25. **a.** Bertchesgarden   **b.** Bertchesgarden   **c.** Berchtesgaden
    (German city)

26. **a.** Tallahatchie   **b.** Tallahachee   **c.** Tallahatchee
    (river in Mississippi)

27. **a.** Chatahoochie   **b.** Chattahoochee   **c.** Chattahoochie
    (river flowing along the boundary of Georgia and Alabama)

28. **a.** Monteviddeo   **b.** Montivideo   **c.** Montevideo
    (Uruguayan city)

29. **a.** Guinnea-Byssau   **b.** Guinea-Byssau   **c.** Guinea-Bissau
    (country of western Africa)

30. **a.** Andemon Islands   **b.** Andemann Islands   **c.** Andaman Islands
    (islands of India in the Bay of Bengal)

31. **a.** Guadlajara   **b.** Guadalajara   **c.** Guadelahara
    (Mexican city)

32. **a.** Pappete   **b.** Papeete   **c.** Pappeet
    (Tahitian port, in the Society Islands of French Polynesia)

33. **a.** Elsmere Island   **b.** Ellsmeer Island   **c.** Ellesmere Island
(Canadian island near Greenland)

34. **a.** Atacama Desert   **b.** Attacamma Desert   **c.** Athacama Desert
(desert in Chile)

35. **a.** Dhaulagiri   **b.** Dhologiri   **c.** Daulaggiri
(Himalayan peak in Nepal, fifth highest mountain in the world)

36. **a.** Irawaddy   **b.** Irrawadi   **c.** Irrawaddy
(river of Myanmar)

37. **a.** Dardonnelles   **b.** Dardanels   **c.** Dardanelles
(Turkish strait between the Sea of Marmara and the Aegean Sea; the Hellespont)

38. **a.** Uttarh Prodesh   **b.** Uttar Pradesch   **c.** Uttar Pradesh
(Indian state bordering Nepal and Tibet)

39. **a.** Rowalpinde   **b.** Rawalpinde   **c.** Rawalpindi
(city of Pakistan)

40. **a.** Sea of Okhotsk   **b.** Sea of Okotzk   **c.** Sea of Okhotzk
(arm of the northern Pacific Ocean near Russia's Kamchatka Peninsula)

41. **a.** Elluthera   **b.** Elleuthera   **c.** Eleuthera
(island of the northern Bahamas)

42. **a.** Ammundsen Sea   **b.** Amundsson Sea   **c.** Amundssen Sea
(sea, part of the southern Pacific Ocean, along coast of Marie Byrd Land, Antarctica)

43. **a.** Kuala Lumpur   **b.** Koala Lumpure   **c.** Kualla Lompure
(Malaysian city)

44. **a.** Okefenokee   **b.** Okefennokee   **c.** Okefennokie

    (extensive swamp of Georgia and Florida)

45. **a.** Tiperrary   **b.** Tipperary   **c.** Tipperrary

    (town and county in the Republic of Ireland)

46. **a.** Matabilliland   **b.** Matabeeliland   **c.** Matabeleland

    (region of southwestern Zimbabwe)

47. **a.** Novosibirsk   **b.** Novasiberske   **c.** Novosibersk

    (Russian city)

48. **a.** Molluccas   **b.** Mollucas   **c.** Moluccas

    (islands of Indonesia in the Malay Archipelago; once the Spice Islands)

49. **a.** Straits of Mackinak **b.** Straits of Mackinac **c.** Straits of Mackinack

    (channel connecting Lake Huron and Lake Michigan)

50. **a.** Bornemouthe   **b.** Bournemouth   **c.** Bournmouthe

    (coastal town in Dorset, southern England)

❀ Say It and Spell It 14

Write in the correct spelling.

1. **boo-yuh-BAYS**   _____

   (rich fish stew)

2. **BEE-buh-lo**   _____

   (small trinket or ornament for the house)

3. KEE-loyd _____
   (spot of thick scar tissue)

4. aw-TAHK-thun-us _____
   (native or indigenous)

5. PER-uh-gee _____
   (orbital point nearest the earth's center)

6. uh-BET-ment _____
   (manifest aiding or supporting)

7. FLIV-er _____
   (cheap old automobile)

8. BIZ-muth _____
   (heavy metallic element used in alloys)

9. suh-RIL-uk _____
   (pertaining to the alphabet of the Russian and other languages)

10. FLAHK-yoo-lunt _____
    (fluffy or woollike)

11. PAHL-ee-wahg _____
    (tadpole)

12. DEK-uh-lahg _____
    (Ten Commandments)

13. SEL-uh-don _____
    (grayish yellow green)

14. ko-ee-VAL-uh-tee   _____

    (being of the same time or period)

15. dis-uh-BEEL   _____

    (state of being carelessly or only partly dressed)

16. sin-fo-nee-ET-uh   _____

    (small symphony orchestra)

17. in-NYOOR   _____

    (to make accepting of or accustomed to)

18. AHN-trakt   _____

    (music, dance, etc., interlude between acts of a play)

19. sep-tyoo-uh-jen-AYR-ee-un   _____

    (one of an age 70–79)

20. JOO-joo   _____

    (African fetish or charm or its purported magical power)

> You must remember that it is permissible for spelling to drive you crazy. Spelling had this effect on Andrew Jackson, who once blew his stack while trying to write a Presidential paper. "It's a damn poor mind that can think of only one way to spell a word!" the President cried.
>
> —John Irving

✿ Three-Word Quizzicles 91–95

The words in each of these wee bees have not been idly chosen.
Write in the correct spelling.

Ninety-one

1. RAHNG-kus _____

   (rattling or whistling sound heard in the chest)

2. CHAHNG-sam _____

   (long mandarin-collared dress with a slit skirt)

3. kahm-SEEN _____

   (Saharan spring southerly wind of Egypt)

Ninety-two

1. uh-SEED-ee-uh _____

   (spiritual apathy or enervation)

2. uh-POR-ee-uh _____

   (rhetorically, expression or feigning of being uncertain or in doubt)

3. uh-set-ul-sal-uh-SIL-ik (acid) _____

   (aspirin)

Ninety-three

1. ay-LAHN vee-TAL   _____
   (the vital force in life)

2. fem-fuh-TAL   _____
   (alluring or dangerous seductive woman)

3. KRAL   _____
   (African village, typically of huts enclosed by a stockade)

Ninety-four

1. ES-ker   _____
   (glacially deposited ridge of coarse gravel)

2. ES-kar   _____
   (scab formed from a burn)

3. JIP-er   _____
   (one who cheats, gouges, or shortchanges another)

Ninety-five

1. BAHB-uh-link   _____
   (migratory American songbird)

2. BAHB-kuh   _____
   (flavored coffee cake)

3. BAHB-uhn   _____
   (reel or spool for spinning, knitting, etc.)

❋ Field Test 2: Fine Arts

Terms from art history, painting, sculpture . . .
   Circle the correct spelling.

1. **a.** pleinairism   **b.** plaineairism   **c.** pleineairism
   (French painting style accenting outdoor, natural light)

2. **a.** DeStyjl   **b.** de Stijll   **c.** de Stijl
   (modern Dutch painting style using primary colors)

3. **a.** churigueresque   **b.** churrigeuresque   **c.** churrigueresque
   (pertaining to the extravagant, detailed Baroque architecture of Spain)

4. **a.** seicennto   **b.** seicento   **c.** seicentto
   (the seventeenth century, especially with regard to Italian art)

5. **a.** sphumma'to   **b.** sfuemato   **c.** sfumato
   (painter's subtle blurring, blending, or softening of outlines)

6. **a.** grisaille   **b.** grizaille   **c.** grissaile
   (style of painting using shades of gray)

7. **a.** entasis   **b.** enthases   **c.** entassis
   (artful "swelling" in classical Greek columns to compensate for concave illusion)

8. **a.** kouros   **b.** khoros   **c.** kourros
   (a Greek sculpture of an upright nude male, especially one pre-fifth century BC)

9. **a.** Phydeas   **b.** Phidias   **c.** Phidius
   (Greek sculptor, flourished fifth century BC)

10. **a.** contreposto   **b.** contraposto   **c.** contrapposto
    (positional depiction of the human body with the upper body turned at an angle)

11. **a.** tennebrism   **b.** tenebrism   **c.** tennabrism

(the seeking or achieving of artful shadow-and-light effects in painting)

12. **a.** Hochusei   **b.** Hokusei   **c.** Hokusai

(Japanese landscape artist and printmaker, 1760–1849)

13. **a.** Mesopatamian   **b.** Mesoppatamian   **c.** Mesopotamian

(pertaining to the ancient Sumer, Babylonian, etc., cultures and art before the Mongols)

14. **a.** uraeus   **b.** eureus   **c.** ureus

(serpent symbol of the ancient Egyptians, depicted on headdresses of rulers and deities)

15. **a.** tympannim   **b.** timpanum   **c.** tympanum

(recessed triangular face of a pediment or between an arch and window or door lintel)

16. **a.** cloasonnée   **b.** cloisonné   **c.** cloissonée

(decorative enamelwork using usually a metal background)

17. **a.** corbel   **b.** korbel   **c.** corbelle

(projecting stone, brick, etc., bracket often to support a cornice or arch)

18. **a.** korbeille   **b.** corbeil   **c.** corbeille

(architectural ornament in the form of a sculpted basket of fruit or flowers)

19. **a.** Prachtsiteles   **b.** Praxsiteles   **c.** Praxiteles

(Athenian sculptor, fl. 370–330 BC)

20. **a.** Turbrughen   **b.** Terbrughan   **c.** Terbrugghen

(Dutch painter, 1588–1629)

21   **a** platteresque   **b.** plateresk   **c.** plateresque

(low-relief ornamentational style of sixteenth-century Spain)

22. **a.** Pisarro   **b.** Pissarro   **c.** Pissaro

(French painter, 1830–1903)

23. **a.** Caravaggio   **b.** Carravaggio   **c.** Carravagio
(Italian painter, 1573–1610)

24. **a.** stele   **b.** stiele   **c.** stielle
(monument or tablet in the form of an upright inscribed or sculpted slab)

25. **a.** stylobate   **b.** steilobate   **c.** stilobate
(foundation of a row of classical columns or colonnade)

26. **a.** gallilee   **b.** galillee   **c.** galilee
(small chapel, porch, or tower vestibule of a medieval English church)

27. **a.** ur-rhythmy   **b.** eurythmy   **c.** eurrhythmy
(architectural harmony of proportions)

28. **a.** Bottacelli   **b.** Botticelli   **c.** Boticelli
(Italian Renaissance painter, 1445–1510)

29. **a.** seilography   **b.** xylography   **c.** zylography
(the art of wood engraving)

30. **a.** triptych   **b.** tryptich   **c.** triptyche
(three side-by-side, often hinged paintings)

❁ Multiple Choice 15

Circle the correct spelling.

1. **a.** odyssies   **b.** oddysseys   **c.** odysseys   **d.** oddyseys
(travels)

2. **a.** shillala   **b.** shilally   **c.** shillelagh   **d.** shellelagh
(Irish cudgel)

3. **a.** whippoorwill   **b.** whipporwill   **c.** whipoorwill   **d.** whipoorwyl
    (nocturnal bird, the goatsucker)

4. **a.** vichisoise   **b.** vichysoisse   **c.** vichyssoise   **d.** vichysoise
    (pureed cold soup)

5. **a.** para-mutual   **b.** pari-mutual   **c.** parimutual   **d.** pari-mutuel
    (betting pool)

6. **a.** sassifrass   **b.** sasifrass   **c.** sasafrass   **d.** sassafras
    (flavorful root bark)

7. **a.** floralegium   **b.** floralegeum   **c.** floraligium   **d.** florilegium
    (collection of writings or anthology)

8. **a.** castinettes   **b.** castanets   **c.** castanettes   **d.** castinets
    (handheld, finger-clapped musical percussion shells)

9. **a.** diosiscan   **b.** diocisan   **c.** dioscesan   **d.** diocesan
    (pertaining to a bishop's jurisdiction)

10. **a.** reredos   **b.** raredos   **c.** rarados   **d.** raradas
    (ornamental wood or stone screen or facing behind an altar)

11. **a.** granary   **b.** grainary   **c.** granery   **d.** grainery
    (grain storehouse)

12. **a.** hulliballoo   **b.** hullibaloo   **c.** hullabaloo   **d.** hulleballo
    (ruckus)

13. **a.** cupie   **b.** kewpee   **c.** kewpie   **d.** cupee
    (chubby doll)

14. **a.** millenneum   **b.** millennium   **c.** millenium   **d.** milennium
    (thousand years)

15. **a.** byalis   **b.** byallies   **c.** bialys   **d.** bialies
(*flat breakfast rolls*)

16. **a.** obeyescence   **b.** obeisance   **c.** obeisence   **d.** obeiscence
(*deference or homage*)

17. **a.** Weimarinor   **b.** Weimaraner   **c.** Whymariner   **d.** Weimariner
(*short-haired German dog breed*)

18. **a.** tinsellerie   **b.** tinselerie   **c.** tinnsillry   **d.** tinselry
(*ornamentation*)

19. **a.** symoleon   **b.** simolion   **c.** simoleon   **d.** simolleon
(*dollar*)

20. **a.** babbushka   **b.** babuschka   **c.** babbuschka   **d.** babushka
(*head kerchief*)

A glaring example of the inadequacies of English spelling appeared in a test given to sixty-four graduate students of journalism at Columbia University. The average was twenty-five misspellings out of seventy-eight words. Typical words used in the test were analogous, dissension, harassed, siege, canoeist, ecstasy, restaurateur, vilification, dietition, guerrilla, supersede, and, appropriately, misspell. Foreign students did better than the native-born, pointing up the advantages of bilingualism. Another series of spellings so ghastly as to be almost unbelievable is submitted by Professor Arnold Hartoch of the Chicago Navy Pier branch of the University of Illinois: dumnb, middnite, lieutendent, wisch, rifel, cowtch, natly (*naturally*), tyered, youniform, sodiers, speach, aliet (*alight*), theirfour, theorhea (*theory*).

—Mario Pei

❀ Five-Word Quizzicles 37–39

The words in each of these wee bees have not been idly chosen.
Write in the correct spelling.

Thirty-seven

1. ter-uh-TAHL-uh-jee   _____

   (study of malformations, birth defects, etc.)

2. tuh-RAIR-ee-um   _____

   (usually glass indoor enclosure for plants or small animals)

3. tor-OO-tiks   _____

   (art of detailed metalworking, as by embossing or chasing)

4. TER-uh-playn   _____

   (level surface or platform for mounting a heavy gun)

5. ter-uh-DOL-uh-jee   _____

   (study of ferns)

One research study is that of Thomas Pollock, of New York University, conducted between 1950 and 1964. In this study, English teachers in high schools and colleges throughout the country reported 90,000 instances of misspellings. But a large percentage of the 90,000 misspellings involved only nine words: their (there), too (to), receive, believe (belief), all right, separate, coming, until, and character.

—Edna L. Furness

Thirty-eight

1. SER-uh-ments   _____

   (burial garments)

2. ser-uh-TO-nin   _____

   (organic compound that is a neurotransmitter and muscle stimulator in mammals)

3. sin-uh-RAR-ee-um   _____

   (repository for the cremated ashes of the dead)

4. suh-RAL-yo   _____

   (harem)

5. suh-NO-tee   _____

   (deep Yucatan limestone sinkhole with water at the bottom)

Thirty-nine

1. hy-AY-tul   _____

   (pertaining to an interval or interruption in continuity)

2. huh-LAHL   _____

   (sanctioned by Islamic law, especially ritually fit food)

3. HY-uh-mal   _____

   (pertaining to winter)

4. HY-uh-tul   _____

   (pertaining to rain)

5. HAL-see-un   _____

   (peacefully ideal, prosperous, or golden)

❁ Fluster Cluster 3

Circle the misspelled words.

The young baron (no mere rotourier), feeling a bit distrait after an inveighing, sobriquet-laced affray in an estominet with his outré fiancée over her assaying too many glasses of Hungarian Toquay and then with a partner dancing a wild paso doble and a careening strathspay—she ricocheted right into a soigné roué—at last summoned a cabriolet driven by a Japanese-speaking Nisei. The baron returned home to enjoy a large parfait and watch an animé narrated in an odd Franglais.

❁ Field Test 3: Natural Sciences

Terms from biology, physics, geology, chemistry, astronomy . . .
   Circle the correct spelling.

1. **a.** aphelion   **b.** appheleon   **c.** aphelion
   (orbital point of a planet, comet, etc., farthest from the sun)

2. **a.** oersted   **b.** ursted   **c.** orsted
   (unit of magnetic intensity in a thermodynamic system)

3. **a.** aurora borialis   **b.** aurura borrealis   **c.** aurora borealis
   (upper-atmospheric radiance occurring in the Northern Hemisphere; northern lights)

4. **a.** baretter   **b.** barretter   **c.** barreter
   (early type of radio detector or controller)

5. **a.** michacious   **b.** micaceous   **c.** micacious
   (containing or resembling mica)

6. **a.** berilleum **b.** berillium **c.** beryllium

   (lightweight rigid metallic element)

7. **a.** gabbrhoic **b.** gabroic **c.** gabbroic

   (composed of a dark granular igneous rock, mostly labradorite and augite)

8. **a.** selinoddessy **b.** selenodesy **c.** selenoddesy

   (study and measurement of the moon's surface and gravitational field)

9. **a.** sapraphite **b.** saprophyte **c.** saprophite

   (organism, such as a fungus, feeding on decaying or dead matter)

10. **a.** cynocyte **b.** coenocite **c.** coenocyte

    (multinucleic cytoplasmic or protoplasmic mass within a single cell wall)

11. **a.** bremmstralung **b.** bremstrallung **c.** bremsstrahlung

    (electromagnetic radiation produced by an accelerating electron)

12. **a.** ecscesis **b.** ecsesis **c.** ecesis

    (immigrant plant's successful establishment as a species in a new environment)

13. **a.** karyogamy **b.** caryogamy **c.** kariogamy

    (fusing of cell nuclei, as in fertilization)

14. **a.** Van de Graff generator **b.** Van de Groff generator **c.** Van de Graaff generator

    (generator of high-voltage static electricity)

15. **a.** teknetium **b.** technetium **c.** technesium

    (radioactive metal, atomic number 43, that is a product of uranium fission)

16. **a.** Boöhtes **b.** Bowotes **c.** Boötes

    (northern constellation between Ursa Major and Serpens: The Herdsman)

17. **a.** Bequerelle   **b.** Becquerel   **c.** Becquerrel

    (*unit of radioactivity in the International System*)

18. **a.** sizygy   **b.** syzygy   **c.** sizsygy

    (*alignment of three celestial bodies*)

19. **a.** Caephid   **b.** Cephid   **c.** Cepheid

    (*star with intrinsic varying brightness*)

20. **a.** skollex   **b.** skolex   **c.** scolex

    (*head of a tapeworm*)

21. **a.** poise   **b.** poighs   **c.** poize

    (*unit of dynamic viscosity*)

22. **a.** dicotyledon   **b.** dycotyledon   **c.** dichotyledon

    (*class of angiospermous plants*)

23. **a.** arillate   **b.** arylate   **c.** arulate

    (*to introduce a certain group into a compound*)

24. **a.** thiksotropy   **b.** thicsotropy   **c.** thixotropy

    (*the turning of gels to liquid when shaken or stirred*)

25. **a.** stoicheometry   **b.** stoikemetry   **c.** stoichiometry

    (*calculation of quantities in chemical reactions*)

26. **a.** quoquoversal   **b.** quaquaversal   **c.** quaquaversile

    (*sloping down on all sides from the center*)

27. **a.** entholpy   **b.** enthalpy   **c.** enthollpy

    (*in a thermodynamic system, the sum of internal energy and the product of its volume and exerted surrounding pressure*)

28. **a.** Pleistocene   **b.** Pliestocene   **c.** Pleisstocene
(epoch of geologic time)

29. **a.** Mischerlich's law   **b.** Mitscherlich's law   **c.** Mitcherlich's law
("isomorphous substances have similar chemical compositions and analogous formulas")

30. **a.** lyeophilize   **b.** liophilize   **c.** lyophilize
(to freeze-dry)

✱ Three-Word Quizzicles 96–100

The words in each of these wee bees have not been idly chosen.
Write in the correct spelling.

Ninety-six

1. **nuh-SEL** _____
   (streamlined enclosure in an aircraft for crew, cargo, an engine, etc.)

2. **FIL-uh-mel** _____
   (nightingale)

3. **muh-REL** _____
   (any of various common edible mushrooms)

Ninety-seven

1. EN-er-vayt

   (to sap the strength of or energy from)

2. uh-NAF-uh-ruh

   (rhetorical repetition of a word or phrase at the beginning of successive clauses, paragraphs, etc.)

3. in-ER-vayt

   (to supply [a body part] with nerves)

Ninety-eight

1. am-uh-RET-o

   (almond-flavored Italian liqueur)

2. in-am-uh-RAH-to

   (beau or male lover)

3. am-uh-RET-o

   (cupid image or figure)

Ninety-nine

1. eh-FEN-dee

   (esteemed prosperous or educated man of the eastern Mediterranean)

2. af-ri-KAHN-er

   (South African of European and especially Dutch ancestry)

3. AH-mun-deen

   (prepared or garnished with almonds)

One Hundred

1. SO-ler PLEK-sus   _____

   (pit of the stomach)

2. an-uh-fuh-LAK-sis   _____

   (extreme sensitivity to a substance following first exposure to it)

3. TMEE-sis   _____

   (separating parts of a word with an inserted word)

✿ Say It and Spell It 15

Write in the correct spelling.

1. seer-o-KYOO-myoo-lus   _____

   (high-altitude cloud form)

2. on-uh-mah-tuh-PEE-uh   _____

   (creation or use of words whose sound evokes their meaning)

3. FLUK-shun   _____

   (a flowing or changing action)

4. POHL-tis   _____

   (soothing or healing soft, often warm mass on cloth applied to a sore)

5. AN-yu-ler   _____

   (ring-shaped or ring forming)

6. jim-DAN-dee   _____

   (wonderful or quite fine)

7. FUS-buj-et-ee   _____

   (fussy or nitpicking)

8. mad-ruh-LEN   _____

   (tomato-flavored consommé)

9. LEJ-er-duh-mayn   _____

   (sleight of hand or skillful, tricky moves)

10. AHK-uh-REE-nuh   _____

    (small finger-holed, somewhat ovoid wind instrument; "sweet potato")

11. fuh-NIK-yu-ler   _____

    (cable railway on an incline)

12. hal-uh-LOO-yuh   _____

    (word used to express joy or thanks)

13. al-luh-LOO-yuh   _____

    (word used to express joy or thanks)

14. puh-PY-rus   _____

    (ancient writing material or document)

15. DIS-er-tay-ter   _____

    (one who discourses learnedly on a subject)

16. pyew-TRES-uh-bul   _____

    (capable of becoming putrid)

17. YOO-ker   _____

    (to cheat, trick, or swindle)

18. no-AY-kee-un   _____

    (pertaining to Noah or to those times)

19. PAHT-sherd   _____

    (excavated pottery fragment)

20. REK-yuh-zen-see   _____

    (defiance of authority or refusal of duty)

❀ Field Test 4: Performing Arts

Terms from the theater and drama, classical music, opera, ballet and dance . . .

Circle the correct spelling.

1. **a.** Annouilh   **b.** Anouilh   **c.** Anouihl

    (French dramatist, 1910–1987)

2. **a.** fiorretura   **b.** fioretura   **c.** fioritura

    (melodic ornamentation)

3. **a.** labbinotation   **b.** labanotation   **c.** labenotation

    (written notational system of dance movement)

4. **a.** cabaletta   **b.** cabbaletta   **c.** caballetta

    (short, simple aria)

5. **a.** mixolydian   **b.** myxolydean   **c.** myxolidean

    (church mode, G to G on the white piano keys)

6. **a.** Aeschylus   **b.** Aeskylos   **c.** Aeschilus
   (Greek dramatist, 525–456 BC)

7. **a.** entrechatte   **b.** entrechâte   **c.** entrechat
   (a ballet jump with a repeated "beating" of the feet in midair)

8. **a.** Khatchaturian   **b.** Khachaturian   **c.** Kachatoriun
   (Russian Armenian-born composer, 1903–1978)

9. **a.** dodekophony   **b.** dodeccaphony   **c.** dodecaphony
   (twelve-tone music)

10. **a.** pascacoglia   **b.** passacaglia   **c.** pasaccaglia
    (seventeenth- or eighteenth-century piece with variations on a ground bass)

11. **a.** neume   **b.** niume   **c.** neome
    (plainsong notational symbols used in Gregorian chant)

12. **a.** hamartia   **b.** hammartia   **c.** hammarcia
    (in drama, a hero's tragic flaw)

13. **a.** cemballoe   **b.** cemballo   **c.** cembalo
    (harpsichord)

14. **a.** ralentando   **b.** rallentando   **c.** rallantando
    (musical direction to slacken tempo; ritardando)

15. **a.** tessitura   **b.** tesattura   **c.** tesitura
    (average vocal or instrumental range of a piece)

16. **a.** zapateado   **b.** zapoteato   **c.** zapadeado
    (in solo flamenco dance, rhythmic stamping or tapping of the feet)

17. **a.** *Così van tutti*   **b.** *Così fan tutte*   **c.** *Così fan tutti*
    (Mozart opera)

18. **a.** mellodeon   **b.** melodion   **c.** melodeon
    (small reed organ or type of accordion)

19. **a.** mellismatic   **b.** melysmatic   **c.** melismatic
    (using vocal melodic embellishment, several notes to one syllable)

20. **a.** Messiaen   **b.** Messiene   **c.** Messiaene
    (French composer and organist, 1908–1992)

21. **a.** sforrzando   **b.** sfforzando   **c.** sforzando
    (emphatically accentuated or stressed)

22. **a.** sfoggato   **b.** sfoggatto   **c.** sfogato
    (light and easy)

23. **a.** Grande Guinol   **b.** Grande Guignol   **c.** Grand Guignolle
    (dramatic performance stressing graphic horror, gore, etc.)

24. **a.** denoumente   **b.** dennoument   **c.** denouement
    (in drama or literature, the plot's climactic resolution or outcome)

25. **a.** Bözindorfer   **b.** Bösendorffer   **c.** Bösendorfer
    (piano whose bass register and keyboard extends to F below the standard A)

26. **a.** Diagheleff   **b.** Diaghillev   **c.** Diaghilev
    (Russian ballet impresario, 1872–1929)

27. **a.** colorateura   **b.** coloretura   **c.** coloratura
    (soprano gifted in light embellishment and lyrical, dazzling virtuoso passages)

28. **a.** descantte   **b.** descante   **c.** descant

(higher-vocal-range contrapuntal melody, usually above the tenor)

29. **a.** Kirchel listing   **b.** Köchel listing   **c.** Kirschel listing

(order-of-composition catalog, chronologically numbered, of Mozart's works)

30. **a.** Gesamtkünstwerk   **b.** Gesamptkunstwerk   **c.** Gesamtkunstwerk

(overall creation of an artist, notably of Wagner, in terms of music, drama, etc.)

❄ Scrabbley Jumble

Rearrange the letters to form a word whose meaning accords with the definition.

1. **adrgams**   _____
   (emerald)

2. **itnacllaeri**   _____
   (lizardlike)

3. **uscaanib**   _____
   (solely utilitarian, practical, or mundane)

4. **sonirfs**   _____
   (palpable thrill, shudder, or excited moment)

5. **esyneltihpeachnr**   _____
   (made of gold and ivory)

6. **eticvscai**   _____
   (drying agent)

7. libincalh

   (swelling or sore caused by cold temperature)

8. osucxaosil

   (living or growing among rocks)

9. iltomla

   (woman's one-piece bathing suit)

10. trimvudeau

    (rule by two)

11. cattyprlhoc

    (one who does brass rubbings)

12. eurmhttaagu

    (magician or miracle worker)

13. dusivinotsciisu

    (marked by changeableness or happenstance)

14. slaideswa

    (offered toasts at a festive drinking occasion)

15. srienececv

    (greenness)

16. olsetcgyahol

    (theological study matters concerning the end of the world)

17. ionsnaittrua

    (renovation or restoration)

18. elaeltnatr

(lively dance of southern Italy)

19. eaayldloodg

(cleverness or originality with words)

20. isztadma

(secret or politically banned literature published underground)

✤ Three-Word Quizzicles 101–105

The words in each of these wee bees have not been idly chosen.
Write in the correct spelling.

One Hundred One

1. kuh-NAHN-ik

(in accordance with accepted, approved, or orthodox literary works)

2. THAHN-ik

(infernal or pertaining to the underworld)

3. mes-ee-AN-ik

(pertaining to an awaited savior or deliverer bringing truth, redemption, etc.)

One Hundred Two

1. MIM-uh-kree _____

   (close imitation, especially in manner, voice, etc.)

2. GIM-uh-kree _____

   (contrivance, method, etc., to accomplish something or get attention)

3. STAT-ik-lee _____

   (in a motionless, inactive, or passive way)

One Hundred Three

1. THER-uh-mun _____

   (high-pitch electronic musical instrument played by hand motions near two antennas)

2. IM-ul-mun _____

   (airplane looping-rolling maneuver to climb and alter direction at the same time)

3. TEL-uh-mun _____

   (in architecture, a sculptural human figure used as a support; atlas)

One Hundred Four

1. uh-FAY-zhuh _____

   (impairment of speech or comprehension due to disease or brain damage)

2. AF-un-pin-sher _____

   (breed of European toy dog with wiry, shaggy hair, erect ears, and a chin tuft)

3. uh-FIS-uh-nul _____

   (available at pharmacies or recognized by a pharmacopoeia)

One Hundred Five

1. KAR-it _____

   (vee-like proofreading symbol used at an insertion)

2. kuh-RAH-tid _____

   (in humans, either of two principal neck arteries)

3. KAR-uh-tee _____

   (bright orange in color or red-haired)

❊ -Able or -Ible 1

Write in the word's (or partial word's) correct adjectival *-able* or *-ible* form.

1.	amass	_____	14. deter	_____
2.	analyze	_____	15. dispense	_____
3.	appease	_____	16. erect	_____
4.	bid	_____	17. excerpt	_____
5.	code	_____	18. exhaust	_____
6.	commit	_____	19. expand	_____
7.	compass	_____	20. gauge	_____
8.	condemn	_____	21. gel	_____
9.	contest	_____	22. impute	_____
10.	corrode	_____	23. indel-	_____
11.	corrupt	_____	24. indubit-	_____
12.	define	_____	25. ingest	_____
13.	degrade	_____		

❁ -Able or -Ible 2

Write in the word's (or partial word's) correct adjectival -*able* or -*ible* form.

1.	interrupt	_____	14.	remit	_____
2.	kiss	_____	15.	resist	_____
3.	lease	_____	16.	salvage	_____
4.	limit	_____	17.	scale	_____
5.	locate	_____	18.	scan	_____
6.	measure	_____	19.	spare	_____
7.	part	_____	20.	submerge	_____
8.	persuade	_____	21.	tithe	_____
9.	please	_____	22.	unbudg-	_____
10.	ponder	_____	23.	unimpeach-	_____
11.	postpone	_____	24.	vanquish	_____
12.	produce	_____	25.	win	_____
13.	refut-	_____			

Spellings in English are so treacherous, and opportunities for flummoxing so abundant, that the authorities themselves sometimes stumble. The first printing of the second edition of Webster's New World Dictionary had millennium spelled millenium in its definition of that word, while in the first edition of the American Heritage Dictionary you can find vichysoisse instead of vichyssoise. In The English Language [page 91], Robert Burchfield, called by William Safire the "world's most influential lexicographer," talks about prescriptivists who regard "innovation as dangerous or at any

❃ Five-Word Quizzicles 40–42

The words in each of these wee bees have not been idly chosen.
Write in the correct spelling.

Forty

1. **puh-LAY-dee-um** _____

   (safeguard or guarantor, as of political rights)

2. **PAL-uh-din** _____

   (chivalrous champion or hero of a cause)

3. **puh-LO-tuh** _____

   (ball used in the game of jai alai)

4. **PAL-uh-nohd** _____

   (poem retracting something expressed in an earlier poem)

5. **PAL-ut** _____

   (narrow hard bed or mattress of straw)

---

rate *resistable*." It should be *resistible*. In The Story of Language, Mario
Pei writes *flectional* on page 114 and *flexional* just four pages later. And in
The Treasure of Our Tongue, Lincoln Barnett laments the decline of spelling by noting: "An English examination at New Jersey's Fairleigh Dickinson
University disclosed that less than one quarter of the freshmen class could
spell *professor* correctly." I wonder, for my part, how many of them could
spell *freshman class*?

—Bill Bryson

Forty-one

1. IL-ee-um

   (terminal part of the small intestine)

   _____

2. IL-ee-um

   (Troy)

   _____

3. IL-ee-um

   (largest of three bones in either half of the pelvis)

   _____

4. UL-ij

   (liquid lost in a bottle, cask, etc., as from leakage)

   _____

5. EYE-lum

   (in big bang theory, matter hypothesized as preceding chemical elements)

   _____

Forty-two

1. kuh-NO-lee

   (tubelike sweet deep-fried pastry)

   _____

2. kuh-PEL-uh

   (bright double star in the constellation Auriga)

   _____

3. kuh-NO-la

   (rapeseed vegetable oil, considered healthful)

   _____

4. kuh-RIG-muh

   (Christian proclaiming of salvation from the Gospels)

   _____

5. KA-nuh-duh

   (Dravidian language of southern India)

   _____

❀ -Able or -Ible 3

Write in the word's (or partial word's) correct adjectival -*able* or -*ible* form.

1. suppress _____
2. address _____
3. confess _____
4. compress _____
5. fuse _____
6. excuse _____
7. infuse _____
8. confuse _____
9. defense _____
10. defend _____
11. censure _____
12. censor _____
13. reverse _____

14. traverse _____
15. invert _____
16. deduct _____
17. conduct _____
18. comprend _____
19. comprehens- _____
20. contract _____
21. intract- _____
22. delect- _____
23. dissect _____
24. effect _____
25. reject _____

❀ Killer Bee 1

Write in the correct spelling.

1. **fy-KAHL-uh-jee** _____

   (study of algae)

2. **fil-uh-RY-uh-sis** _____

   (disease from infestation by elongated worms)

3. **fuh-LOO-kuh** _____

   (swift Mediterranean lateen-rigged sailing vessel)

4. **fuh-LOOM-uh-nist** _____

   (collector of matchbooks, matchboxes, etc.)

5. **flo-JIS-tun** _____

   (ancient supposed "material" of fire)

6. **fil-HEL-un** _____

   (one who admires Greece or the Greeks)

7. **fy-LET-ik** _____

   (pertaining to an organism's developmental change in evolutionary descent)

8. **FAZ-mid** _____

   (any of the order that includes leaf insects or walking sticks)

9. **fyoo-LIJ-uh-nus** _____

   (soot-colored, dark, or obscure)

10. **FAL-uh-rohp** _____

    (small wading bird whose toes enable it to swim)

❁ Killer Bee 2

Write in the correct spelling.

1. **PAR-uh-did-ul** _____

   (alternating-hands drumbeat pattern slower than a drumroll)

2. **PER-ee-apt** _____

   (amulet)

3. **par-uh-no-MAS-tik** _____

   (characterized by wordplay or punning)

4. **puh-RAH-nuh-mus** _____

   (having the same word root or derivation)

5. **PEER-uh-form** _____

   (pear-shaped)

6. **PEER-uh-nist** _____

   (extreme or radical skeptic)

7. **py-RO-sis** _____

   (heartburn)

8. **PAR-ee pas-OO** _____

   (at an equal rate or pace)

9. **PAR-kuh-tree** _____

   (surface of often geometric inlaid wood, as in floors)

10. **puh-RAHZ-mee-uh** _____

    (distorted or illusory sense of smell)

✿ Killer Bee 3

Write in the correct spelling.

1. **TRO-kee** _____

   (lozenge)

2. **NOO-bee** _____

   (newcomer, especially an Internet novice)

3. **SIS-tuh-lee** _____

   (rhythmic contraction of the heart, as measured in blood pressure)

4. **SHAM-ee** _____

   (small goatlike antelope of mountainous Europe)

5. **SKIP-er-kee** _____

   (Belgian breed of stocky black tailless dog with pointy ears)

6. **TRO-kee** _____

   (metrical foot, a long or stressed syllable followed by a short or unstressed one)

7. **AH-tee** _____

   (Greek goddess of foolhardiness and rashness)

8. **buh-KAN-tee** _____

   (votary or priestess of the Greek god of wine)

9. **TOR-ee-ee** _____

   (iconic Japanese gateway, as to a Shinto shrine)

10. **ay-TWEE** _____

    (small ornamental case, as for sewing needles)

❁ Killer Bee 4

Write in the correct spelling.

1. **kwa-kee-YOO-tul** _____

   (Native American people of the coastal Northwest)

2. **kwahd-ruh-FAHN-ik** _____

   (pertaining to a four-channel sound system)

3. **KWAHN-dum** _____

   (former or erstwhile)

4. KWAHN-sit   _____

   (semicircular prefabricated shelter of corrugated metal)

5. kwa-DREE-uh   _____

   (matador's assistants in a bullfight)

6. KWAH-kuh   _____

   (small coast-dwelling wallaby of Australia)

7. KWAHD-lib-et   _____

   (philosophical or theological point as an issue for debate)

8. kwahsh-ee-OR-kor   _____

   (protein deficiency disease especially affecting children in the third world)

9. kwink-EN-ee-um   _____

   (period of five years; lustrum)

10. kwahd-ruh-sil-AB-ik   _____

    (having four syllables)

❈ Killer Bee 5

Write in the correct spelling.

1. suh-RO-sis   _____

   (women's club or society)

2. sy-LO-sis   _____

   (hair loss)

3. suh-RO-sis   _____

   (disease of citrus trees)

4. suh-RY-uh-sis   _____
   (skin disease)

5. suh-RO-sis   _____
   (fleshy multiple fruit found within the pineapple and mulberry)

6. suh-RY-uh-sis   _____
   (sunstroke)

7. SEER-ee-us   _____
   (small cactus of the western United States and tropical America)

8. si-tuh-KO-sis   _____
   (disease of birds to which humans are susceptible)

9. sis-tuh-ser-KO-sis   _____
   (disease caused by infestation of tapeworm larvae)

10. SEER-ee-us   _____
    (bright star of the constellation Canis Major; the Dog Star)

The Answers

SPELLING WARM-UP 1, PAGE 33

1. a. gumption
2. a. gallivant
3. a. mischievous
4. a. introvert
5. b. homage
6. a. aching
7. a. vassal
8. b. laryngitis
9. a. excerpt
10. b. pittance
11. a. gizzard
12. b. scintillating
13. b. absorption
14. b. exhilaration
15. b. appraisal
16. a. vacuum
17. b. superintendent
18. a. separate
19. b. tariff
20. b. privilege

SPELLING WARM-UP 2, PAGE 33

1. c. heterogeneity
2. c. ancillary
3. a. casuistry
4. c. malaise
5. b. undescried
6. a. beatific
7. c. satiety
8. b. chicanery
9. c. frangible
10. c. taiga
11. b. cutaneous
12. a. desuetude
13. a. millipede
14. a. paucity
15. a. bucolic
16. a. capillary
17. a. ubiquitous
18. a. apogee
19. c. seismometer
20. a. onerous

SPELLING WARM-UP 3, PAGE 34

1. a. antihistamine
2. a. heifer
3. a. agglomeration
4. c. panacea
5. c. cataclysm
6. b. talisman
7. a. vellum
8. b. apothecary
9. b. affidavit
10. c. tocsin
11. a. codicil
12. b. aberration
13. c. cynosure
14. b. denizen
15. a. lagniappe
16. b. apiary
17. d. fascicle
18. a. viand
19. b. acquiescent
20. b. malediction

THREE-WORD QUIZZICLES 1–5, PAGE 35

One	1. carioca	2. caracole	3. karaoke
Two	1. tutu	2. froufrou	3. muumuu
Three	1. aplomb	2. cardamom	3. modicum
Four	1. sludgy	2. jowly	3. chancy
Five	1. truncheon	2. pidgin	3. Cajun

MULTIPLE CHOICE 1, PAGE 37

1. d. deliquesce
2. a. hoi polloi
3. d. diphthongal
4. d. parasol
5. a. litterateur
6. b. latchet
7. d. cerulean
8. c. palimpsest
9. d. craquelure
10. b. rheostat
11. d. farina
12. c. paparazzi
13. b. parure
14. b. inchoate
15. b. cuneiform
16. c. myrmidon
17. a. kaleidoscopic
18. c. megillah
19. d. mah-jongg
20. b. bêtise

WORD AND DEFINITION MATCH 1, PAGE 39

1. r
2. o
3. g
4. i
5. k
6. l
7. h
8. a
9. d
10. t
11. b
12. q
13. s
14. c
15. j
16. f
17. n
18. e
19. m
20. p

FIVE-WORD QUIZZICLES 1–3, PAGE 41

One	1. aqueduct	2. aquifer	3. aquavit	4. aquiline	5. aqueous
Two	1. chorine	2. beguine	3. vitrine	4. damascene	5. terrene
Three	1. gondolier	2. sonneteer	3. pistoleer	4. lavaliere, lavalliere	5. belvedere

SAY IT AND SPELL IT 1, PAGE 43

1. Mardi Gras
2. outlier
3. sapphire
4. willfully
5. willfulness
6. Uruguay
7. transmissible
8. gelée
9. treacly
10. turtlet
11. formatter
12. abysmal
13. perspicacious
14. anneal
15. paraph
16. braised
17. macadam
18. discomfiter
19. carrel, carrell
20. anodyne

FLUSTER CLUSTER 1, PAGE 45

There are six misspellings in the passage: celleret, bankettes, Lette, au faite, annisette, and nonnet. The correct spellings of these words are cellarette or cellaret, banquettes, Lett, au fait, anisette, and nonet.

THREE-WORD QUIZZICLES 6–10, PAGE 45

Six	1. rococo	2. piccolo	3. peccadillo
Seven	1. Methuselah	2. Scheherazade, Scheherezade	3. Agamemnon
Eight	1. tamale	2. timbales	3. tomalley
Nine	1. bacchanal	2. barracuda	3. baccarat
Ten	1. lineament	2. liniment	3. Linnaean, Linnean

TWO WORDS OR ONE 1, PAGE 47

1. snowball
2. taillight
3. backseat
4. redbrick
5. wastewater
6. salesclerk
7. filmmaker
8. pot holder
9. birdbath
10. hair shirt
11. locker room
12. tollbooth
13. stepladder
14. nightclub
15. bow tie
16. barbell
17. hammerlock
18. lawsuit
19. windowsill
20. peephole
21. artwork
22. paper clip
23. pocketknife
24. seabird
25. lamppost

MULTIPLE CHOICE 2, PAGE 48

1. b. sinsemilla
2. c. amercing
3. c. formaldehyde
4. c. pizzicato
5. b. bassinet
6. b. farinaceous
7. c. hobbledehoy
8. b. cicada
9. c. temerarious
10. c. amethyst
11. a. Pocahontas
12. d. melanoma
13. d. cacophony
14. d. filament
15. b. sumpter
16. d. tambourine
17. c. proselyte
18. c. bourgeoise
19. c. brassard
20. d. tsetse fly

DOUBLED LETTER OR NO, PAGE 50

1. misspelling
2. pastime
3. nighttime
4. poetaster
5. drunkenness
6. coattail
7. morass
8. occurrence
9. withhold
10. dumbbell
11. newsstand
12. duress
13. misshapen
14. threshold
15. bookkeeper
16. roommate
17. headdress
18. musketeer
19. teammate
20. suddenness
21. accommodate
22. commemorate
23. necessity
24. pusillanimous
25. commitment

THREE-WORD QUIZZICLES 11–15, PAGE 51

Eleven	1. hegemony	2. anemone	3. hominy
Twelve	1. wainwright	2. acolyte	3. blatherskite
Thirteen	1. Lilliputian	2. picayune	3. pygmaean, pygmean
Fourteen	1. colossus	2. Brobdingnagian	3. googol
Fifteen	1. cannikin	2. baldachin	3. pemmican

SAY IT AND SPELL IT 2, PAGE 53

1. distal
2. amanuenses
3. Baedeker
4. glary
5. dialysis
6. toboggan
7. patroon
8. caitiff
9. prescient
10. tetanus
11. commedia dell'arte
12. imprest
13. pinochle
14. oxidization
15. nuncupative
16. dun
17. twiny
18. kibitzer
19. proselytize
20. cocoon

FIVE-WORD QUIZZICLES 4–6, PAGE 55

Four	1. williwaw	2. foofaraw	3. gewgaw	4. trough	5. kowtow
Five	1. solstitial	2. interspatial	3. surficial	4. carapacial	5. seneschal
Six	1. frippery	2. bain-marie	3. potpourri	4. congeries	5. corroboree

TWO SPELLINGS ALLOWED, PAGE 57

1. aneurysm, aneurism
2. bourne, bourn
3. caravansary, caravanserai
4. tumbrel, tumbril
5. wisenheimer, weisenheimer
6. syllabub, sillabub
7. Manichean, Manichaean
8. absinthe, absinth
9. barcarolle, barcarole
10. janissary, janizary
11. teetotaler, teetotaller
12. cockamamie, cockamamy
13. kaput, kaputt
14. moniker, monicker
15. whodunnit, whodunit
16. tarboosh, tarbush
17. appanage, apanage
18. topee, topi
19. veranda, verandah
20. syrupy, sirupy

MULTIPLE CHOICE 3, PAGE 59

1. b. flytier
2. a. ensorcellment
3. a. carrefour
4. a. jalapeño
5. c. Rorschach
6. c. strychnine
7. d. bimillenary
8. c. Chihuahua
9. d. chatelaine
10. a. cocotte
11. d. skedaddle
12. a. bizarrerie
13. c. naiad
14. c. tae kwon do
15. c. aeolian
16. b. picaresque
17. a. banquette
18. a. koine
19. a. anopheles
20. d. Aesculapian

THREE-WORD QUIZZICLES 16–20, PAGE 61

	1.	2.	3.
Sixteen	ribald	kobold	caterwauled
Seventeen	carafe	cenotaph	shandygaff
Eighteen	geodesy	theodicy	pleurisy
Nineteen	balalaika	violoncello	didgeridoo, djeridoo
Twenty	cosmogony	polygyny	ontogeny

TO BEE—OR NOT TO B, PAGE 63

1. cee	6. jay	11. pee	16. vee
2. dee	7. kay, ka	12. cue	17. double-u, double-you
3. ef	8. el, ell	13. ar	18. ex
4. gee	9. em	14. ess, es	19. wye, wy
5. aitch	10. en	15. tee	20. zee

FIVE-WORD QUIZZICLES 7–9, PAGE 64

Seven	1. khaki	2. ginkgo, gingko	3. gecko	4. Gandhi	5. Gurkha
Eight	1. sashay	2. sachet	3. inveigh	4. distrait	5. coryphée
Nine	1. ratchety	2. crotchety	3. muckety-muck	4. rickety	5. lickety-split

SAY IT AND SPELL IT 3, PAGE 66

1. devoirs	6. tutelage	11. decedent	16. shallot
2. conferee	7. courturière	12. lovey-dovey	17. excursus
3. mucilage	8. soigné, soignée	13. peripatetic	18. frangipani
4. serried	9. chifforobe	14. Judaism	19. gallimaufry
5. muesli	10. gymkhana	15. flotilla	20. psephology

WORD AND DEFINITION MATCH 2, PAGE 68

1. d	6. e	11. i	16. s
2. a	7. c	12. t	17. g
3. q	8. r	13. k	18. h
4. l	9. o	14. n	19. b
5. m	10. f	15. j	20. p

THREE-WORD QUIZZICLES 21–25, PAGE 69

Twenty-one	1. cutlet	2. cuttable	3. cutability
Twenty-two	1. antimacassar	2. macaque	3. mystagogue
Twenty-three	1. kudu, koodoo	2. kudzu	3. kazoo
Twenty-four	1. placard	2. placket	3. plaque
Twenty-five	1. cacciatore	2. cacao	3. kakistocracy

MULTIPLE CHOICE 4, PAGE 71

1. d. moiety
2. c. solfeggio
3. a. parallelism
4. d. manacle
5. c. bonsai
6. b. flibbertigibbety
7. c. stiletto
8. b. tinnitus
9. c. triceratops
10. c. phooey
11. d. scurrilous
12. d. bathyscaphe, bathyscaph
13. c. Sasquatch
14. d. senhor
15. d. tourniquet
16. d. falafel, felafel
17. d. bissextile
18. a. hubbub
19. c. laudanum
20. c. Huguenot

FIVE-WORD QUIZZICLES 10–12, PAGE 73

Ten	1. Appaloosa	2. chaparral	3. palomino	4. calaboose	5. caballero
Eleven	1. offal	2. fo'c'sle	3. wassail	4. dactyl	5. treadle
Twelve	1. dachas	2. otiose	3. missish	4. knish	5. piceous

TWO WORDS OR ONE 2, PAGE 75

1. keypad
2. dartboard
3. pillowcase
4. redshift
5. role model
6. snuffbox
7. mess kit
8. loanword
9. pinsetter
10. place mat
11. legroom
12. night soil
13. riverbank
14. sundial
15. lumberyard
16. tongue twister
17. landmass
18. upper hand
19. flyspeck
20. horselaugh
21. pit stop
22. key chain
23. key ring
24. watercraft
25. master class

SAY IT AND SPELL IT 4, PAGE 76

1. intercalate	6. caisson	11. caparison	16. dahlia
2. fianchetto	7. rapprochement	12. entremets	17. ignis fatuus
3. jonquil	8. episcopate	13. shaman	18. shibboleth
4. zwieback	9. sempiternal	14. alopecia	19. bellwether
5. hibachi	10. scuttlebutt	15. seine	20. thurifer

THREE-WORD QUIZZICLES 26–30, PAGE 78

Twenty-six	1. eyelet	2. aye-aye	3. aglet
Twenty-seven	1. petitpoint	2. pettifoggery	3. patty-cake, pat-a-cake
Twenty-eight	1. meringue	2. merengue, méringue	3. moraine
Twenty-nine	1. erythrism	2. erethism	3. eurhythmy, eurythmy
Thirty	1. Tartarean	2. Tartarian	3. tartarous

ACCENT MARK OR NONE, PAGE 80

1. mañana	7. Götterdämmerung	14. émigré, emigré	20. gemütlichkeit
2. dojo	8. dolce vita	15. crèche	21. forte
3. caïque	9. mano a mano	16. lèse majesté	22. kielbasa
4. panache	10. crêpe suzette	17. objet d'art	23. tête-à-tête
5. arrivederci	11. ouzo	18. aperçu	24. dacha
6. porte-cochère, porte-cochere	12. zabaglione	19. ciao	25. machismo
	13. déjà vu		

MULTIPLE CHOICE 5, PAGE 82

1. c. catechumen	7. d. malapropos	13. c. centenary	18. c. glazier
2. d. menorah	8. b. milquetoast	14. d. boutonniere, boutonnière	19. b. aniline
3. d. conniption	9. c. measly		20. c. meerschaum
4. d. scintilla	10. b. shilly-shallier	15. b. sequelae	
5. a. fierier	11. c. braille	16. c. baccalaureate	
6. a. trichinosis	12. d. debouch	17. a. poultice	

ONE-SYLLABLE WORDS, PAGE 84

1. banns
2. sieve
3. queue
4. xyst
5. brougham
6. phlox
7. nous
8. taupe
9. dhow
10. drought
11. gneiss
12. myrhh
13. putsch
14. knur
15. cloche
16. deign
17. tryst
18. ruche
19. phiz
20. shirr
21. luff
22. conch
23. trough
24. quire
25. boite

THREE-WORD QUIZZICLES 31–35, PAGE 87

Thirty-one	1. onyx	2. aurochs	3. lummox
Thirty-two	1. humus	2. hummus	3. heigh-ho
Thirty-three	1. troubadour	2. Minotaur	3. minatory
Thirty-four	1. peccary	2. peccavi	3. pecuniary
Thirty-five	1. scarab	2. carob	3. caribe

SAY IT AND SPELL IT 5, PAGE 89

1. chicanery
2. simpatico
3. wickiup
4. culotte
5. depilate
6. cul-de-sac
7. Pollyanna
8. accrual
9. hookah
10. vying
11. patrilineal
12. bibliolater
13. hairbreadth, hairsbreadth
14. effervesces
15. curvature
16. crocheter
17. teleology
18. pantywaist
19. tantivy
20. teetotum

FIVE-WORD QUIZZICLES 13–15, PAGE 91

Thirteen	**1.** filiopietism	**2.** philately	**3.** phylactery	**4.** fillip	**5.** fylfot
Fourteen	**1.** bouzouki	**2.** kerflooey	**3.** aioli	**4.** salmagundi	**5.** agouti
Fifteen	**1.** diaeresis, dieresis	**2.** diesis	**3.** diocese	**4.** diuresis	**5.** diaphoresis

NO, NO, NO—YES! 1, PAGE 93

1. bacillus
2. botfly
3. chasuble
4. schmierkase
5. kepi
6. batik
7. wampum
8. nougat
9. tattersall
10. yarmulke
11. lachrymose
12. bedizen
13. apparatchik
14. croupier
15. obloquy
16. chintziness
17. aleatory
18. Xanadu
19. baobab
20. easel
21. leprechaun
22. dyspnea
23. antediluvian
24. staphylococcus
25. eclogue

MULTIPLE CHOICE 6, PAGE 95

1. b. palazzo
2. d. chautauqua
3. a. espadrille
4. a. narcissist
5. c. paraquat
6. c. Naugahyde
7. c. encryption
8. d. Cantabrigian
9. b. Szechuan, Szechwan, Sichuan
10. d. abscise
11. a. salaam
12. b. habeas corpus
13. d. commissary
14. d. catafalque
15. c. Afrikaans
16. a. paramountcy
17. c. generalissimo
18. b. balustrade
19. c. passel
20. d. herculean

THREE-WORD QUIZZICLES 36–40, PAGE 97

Thirty-six	**1.** catarrh	**2.** sitar	**3.** parterre
Thirty-seven	**1.** tsunami	**2.** xebec	**3.** zugzwang
Thirty-eight	**1.** accessible	**2.** assessable	**3.** ascribable
Thirty-nine	**1.** sgraffito	**2.** tangelo	**3.** zucchetto
Forty	**1.** pelage	**2.** pellicle	**3.** pelagic

SPELL IT OUT, PAGE 99

1. pianoforte
2. cabriolet
3. pantaloons
4. mobile vulgus
5. geneva
6. brigantine
7. raspberry
8. wienerwurst
9. synchronization
10. Buncombe County, NC
11. paternoster
12. rumbullion
13. cinematograph
14. ad libitum
15. public house
16. facsimile
17. spatterdashes
18. perquisite
19. veterinarian
20. modulator-demodulator

SAY IT AND SPELL IT 6, PAGE 100

1. birdieing
2. canniness
3. styptic
4. caravel
5. evanescing
6. murmuration
7. bivouacking
8. ululate
9. granite
10. billet
11. conquistador
12. dumdum
13. dum-dum
14. topaz
15. olio
16. tinniness
17. auld lang syne
18. terra-cotta
19. lapful
20. duress

SPELL THE PLURAL, PAGE 102

1. autos-da-fé
2. patresfamilias
3. courts-martial
4. heirs apparent
5. quorums
6. stases
7. billets-doux
8. coccyges, coccyxes
9. anni mirabilis
10. kohlrabies
11. women's rooms
12. klezmorim
13. beaux-esprits
14. pince-nez
15. metastases
16. mots justes
17. goosefoots
18. menservants
19. oyesses
20. chassis
21. beaux gestes, beau gestes
22. nouveaux riches
23. soliloquies
24. bêtes noires
25. modi operandi

THREE-WORD QUIZZICLES 41–45, PAGE 105

Forty-one   1. pekoe   2. furbelow   3. guyot
Forty-two   1. suable   2. subduable   3. pursuable
Forty-three 1. habiliments   2. jipijapa   3. hippety-hop, hippity-hop
Forty-four   1. orrery   2. oriflamme   3. ordonnance
Forty-five   1. clippety-clop 2. harum-scarum   3. niminy-piminy

MULTIPLE CHOICE 7, PAGE 107

1. d. cicerone	6. a. terete	11. b. brummagem	16. c. ziggurat
2. a. inamorata	7. a. gutta-percha	12. c. penicillin	17. d. icicle
3. b. sebaceous	8. b. ytterbium	13. c. hors d'oeuvres	18. a. tam-o'-shanter
4. b. cranny	9. d. silhouette	14. a. syllabary	19. b. trivet
5. b. colossal	10. c. glutenous	15. c. galoshes	20. c. succotash

FIVE-WORD QUIZZICLES 16–18, PAGE 109

Sixteen	1. hymnody	2. suavity	3. quixotry	4. laity	5. comity
Seventeen	1. isostasy	2. isosceles	3. Anglice	4. lieutenancy	5. piquancy
Eighteen	1. elixir	2. pinafore	3. avatar	4. semaphore	5. polyhistor

NO, NO, NO—YES! 2, PAGE 111

1. cicatrix	8. battalion	14. pasteurize	21. maenad
2. discombobulate	9. dromedary	15. tupelo	22. narghile, nargileh
3. oleander	10. astrakhan,	16. maraschino	23. revetment,
4. divagation	astrachan	17. terrazzo	revêtement
5. hebdomadal	11. inveigle	18. phantasmagoria	24. chrysalis
6. eucalyptus	12. molasses	19. Tagalog	25. anise
7. chichi	13. enthymeme	20. gigolo	

SAY IT AND SPELL IT 7, PAGE 113

1. isthmus	6. bated	11. shoofly	16. sclaff
2. passe-partout	7. caffeine	12. abutment	17. Wedgwood
3. hymeneal	8. accruement	13. acned	18. missilery, missilry
4. phthisic	9. statolatry	14. mai-tai	19. décolletage
5. beleaguerment	10. zombiism	15. galoot	20. hawser

THREE-WORD QUIZZICLES 46–50, PAGE 115

Forty-six	1. Pyrrhic	2. piebald	3. pier glass
Forty-seven	1. traipse	2. dais	3. japes
Forty-eight	1. opossum	2. noisome	3. crissum
Forty-nine	1. filicide	2. faille	3. phial
Fifty	1. tondo	2. tournedos	3. rondeau

-IOUS OR -EOUS, PAGE 117

The misspelled words are 2, 5, 8, 10, 11, 12, 13, and 14; their correct spellings are rampageous, deleterious, beauteous, extraneous, veracious, obsequious, vitreous, and ignominious.

MULTIPLE CHOICE 8, PAGE 118

1. c. kohlrabi	6. b. glockenspiel	11. b. talcky	16. d. affidavit
2. d. phylogeny	7. c. Dramamine	12. c. ipecac	17. b. hemorrhage
3. b. acidophilus	8. b. doily	13. d. bludgeon	18. c. cappuccino
4. a. semaphore	9. c. calamine	14. d. poinsettia	19. c. Capuchin
5. d. piccalilli	10. a. tergiversate	15. c. terpsichorean	20. a. obelisk

FIVE-WORD QUIZZICLES 19–21, PAGE 120

Nineteen	1. inveigle	2. allee	3. whey-faced	4. heyday	5. duvet
Twenty	1. portcullis	2. trellis	3. rictus	4. chrysalis	5. cockatrice
Twenty-one	1. spillway	2. bulwark	3. belfry	4. helotry	5. miliary

MEGA MULTIPLE CHOICE, PAGE 122

1. f. appoggiatura	4. a. Hephaestus	7. g. bilirubin	9. b. clepsydra
2. e. Cassiopeia	5. e. boeotian	8. d. apophyge	10. d. succedaneum
3. d. erysipelas	6. b. seppuku		

THREE-WORD QUIZZICLES 51–55, PAGE 123

Fifty-one	1. tarboosh, tarbush	2. farouche	3. ragout
Fifty-two	1. cru	2. cruse	3. krewe
Fifty-three	1. pis aller	2. piezometer	3. specie
Fifty-four	1. ack-ack	2. bric-a-brac	3. dik-dik
Fifty-five	1. termagant	2. unguent	3. viscount

SAY IT AND SPELL IT 8, PAGE 125

1. seminal	6. deferment	11. vitriol	16. wall-less
2. damfool	7. stupefy	12. conferral	17. guttural
3. commemorate	8. exophthalmic	13. rivulet	18. owlet
4. playwright	9. sekt	14. lintel	19. armature
5. anoint	10. consentaneous	15. oppugn	20. freshet

-IE OR -EI, PAGE 127

1. weird	8. forfeit	15. ceiling	22. Siegfried Line
2. sheikh	9. geisha	16. fiefdom	23. kielbasa
3. fiend	10. weir	17. wield	24. lieder
4. skein	11. codeine	18. conceive	25. heinous
5. frieze	12. caffeine	19. receipt	
6. deceive	13. sieve	20. retrieve	
7. seize	14. siege	21. niece	

MULTIPLE CHOICE 9, PAGE 128

1. b. phatic	6. c. svelteness	11. b. bicentenary	16. c. Antaean
2. d. tintinnabulation	7. a. foie gras	12. b. mallet	17. c. littoral
3. a. placket	8. b. genealogically	13. d. abacuses	18. d. acetylene
4. a. daguerreotype	9. b. panegyric	14. a. rimy	19. d. catenary
5. a. rutabaga	10. b. tatterdemalion	15. b. chakra	20. d. fedora

THREE-WORD QUIZZICLES 56–60, PAGE 130

Fifty-six	1. Plimsoll	2. pistole	3. parol
Fifty-seven	1. anile	2. enisle	3. enophile, oenophile
Fifty-eight	1. belletrist	2. bel canto	3. belladonna
Fifty-nine	1. microfiche	2. quiche	3. baksheesh
Sixty	1. quirt	2. QWERTY	3. cuirass

BRITISH SPELLING, PAGE 132

1. aeon	6. pretence	11. analyse	16. furore
2. haemorrhage	7. manoeuvre	12. councillor	17. connexion
3. kerb	8. anaemic	13. aluminium	18. harbour
4. speciality	9. annexe	14. smoulder	19. enrolment
5. pyjamas	10. favourite	15. waggon	20. liquorice

FIVE-WORD QUIZZICLES 22–24, PAGE 133

Twenty-two	1. jalousie	2. synonymy	3. coxcombry	4. facetiae	5. nepenthe
Twenty-three	1. binnacle	2. missal	3. dottle	4. weevil	5. gambrel
Twenty-four	1. tenon	2. sporran	3. rosin	4. tannin	5. guerdon

SAY IT AND SPELL IT 9, PAGE 135

1. deserts	6. intendance	11. pro tem	16. lensless
2. meridional	7. pittance	12. divvied	17. funereal
3. comestible	8. plumy	13. infinitesimal	18. parricide
4. obstreperous	9. shooed	14. sororal	19. harebrained
5. consensual	10. avalanche	15. phaeton	20. singer

-ANCE OR -ENCE / -ANT OR -ENT, PAGE 137

1. aberrance	8. connivance	15. lieutenant	22. preponderant
2. sufferance	9. antecedent	16. intermittent	23. retardant
3. resplendent	10. relevant	17. attractant	24. disputant
4. impedance	11. subsistence	18. decadent	25. adherent
5. cognizant	12. opulence	19. decedent	
6. despondent	13. dalliance	20. defendant	
7. petulance	14. admittance	21. penchant	

THREE-WORD QUIZZICLES 61–65, PAGE 137

Sixty-one	1. merlon	2. guidon	3. midden
Sixty-two	1. baize	2. Cockaigne	3. peignoir
Sixty-three	1. faits accomplis	2. fetor	3. fête champêtre
Sixty-four	1. pigeon	2. stygian	3. misprision
Sixty-five	1. mewl	2. pule	3. shul

MULTIPLE CHOICE 10, PAGE 139

1. c. nyctalopia	6. b. prestidigitator	12. a. homburg	18. b. colophon
2. c. adenoidal	7. b. spinet	13. c. borborygmus	19. b. ptomaine
3. a. chameleon	8. b. usquebaugh	14. b. passementerie	20. d. trekker
4. b. archipelago	9. a. brisket	15. a. ethnogeny	
5. a. bougainvillea, bougainvillaea	10. c. demurral	16. c. dilatation	
	11. c. minaret	17. a. garret	

NO, NO, NO—YES! 3, PAGE 141

1. Beelzebub	8. mariachi	15. antonomasia	22. amaryllis
2. mistletoe	9. adscititious	16. Sisyphean	23. diphtheria
3. gouache	10. plankton	17. susurrus	24. antihistamine
4. propaedeutic	11. cemeteries	18. labanotation	25. griot
5. myrrh	12. quinquennium	19. kitsch	
6. chicle	13. empyrean	20. stevedore	
7. shrapnel	14. picador	21. spermaceti	

FIVE-WORD QUIZZICLES 25–27, PAGE 144

Twenty-five	1. pastiche	2. pasties	3. patisseries	4. paisleys	5. pastis
Twenty-six	1. cyclamen	2. sycophant	3. sciolism	4. seidel	5. zydeco
Twenty-seven	1. colporteur	2. Psalter	3. clangor	4. ordure	5. langur

SAY IT AND SPELL IT 10, PAGE 146

1. gibbet	6. paroxysmal	11. doughty	16. galluses
2. trier	7. matriliny	12. expatriatism	17. papeterie
3. tulle	8. oeuvre	13. antically	18. esophageal
4. maraca	9. peaked	14. trousseau	19. laissez-faireism
5. surveil	10. platen	15. aerify	20. hootenanny

FLUSTER CLUSTER 2, PAGE 148

There are four misspellings in the passage: impune, Khartum, piccayune, and jujune. The correct spellings of these words are impugn, Khartoum, picayune, and jejune.

THREE-WORD QUIZZICLES 66–70, PAGE 148

Sixty-six	1. hippopotamus	2. pseudonymous	3. callus
Sixty-seven	1. horehound	2. hornblende	3. hypnoid
Sixty-eight	1. duodenum	2. molybdenum	3. paronym
Sixty-nine	1. madeleine	2. Mahdism	3. madrilene
Seventy	1. balaclava	2. baklava	3. latke

-OS OR -OES, PAGE 150

1. kimonos	8. farragoes	15. sopranos	22. fiascoes
2. fungoes	9. caballeros	16. vetoes	23. bassos
3. gringos	10. fatsoes	17. pistachios	24. hidalgos
4. fandangos	11. majordomos	18. potatoes	25. bozos
5. lingoes	12. boleros	19. tomatoes	
6. jingoes	13. curios	20. embryos	
7. heroes	14. albinos	21. seraglios	

MULTIPLE CHOICE 11, PAGE 151

1. d. pomegranate	6. b. aneroid	11. c. caoutchouc	16. c. beriberi
2. a. nimiety	7. b. roentgen, röntgen	12. c. monadnock	17. d. fluorescent
3. d. decennary	8. b. Armageddon	13. d. vermeil	18. a. rhadamanthine
4. a. brusquerie	9. c. paralogism	14. c. pharaoh	19. d. niccolic
5. d. bituminous	10. a. velleity	15. c. verrucose	20. c. shekel

FIVE-WORD QUIZZICLES 28–30, PAGE 153

Twenty-eight	1. dissever	2. dissymmetry	3. dysrhythmia	4. desideratum	5. dyspepsia
Twenty-nine	1. hummock	2. tilak	3. dybbuk	4. sapphic	5. tarmac
Thirty	1. amontillado	2. mozzarrella	3. pullulate	4. balbriggan	5. camarilla

CLASSIC CONFUSERS, PAGE 155

1. anoint	6. ecstasy	11. putrefy	16. sacrilegious
2. inoculate	7. idiosyncrasy	12. dilettante	17. supersede
3. desiccate	8. rococo	13. consensus	18. impresario
4. concomitant	9. minuscule	14. liaison	19. obbligato
5. asinine	10. moccasin	15. pavilion	20. de rigueur

SAY IT AND SPELL IT 11, PAGE 156

1. weest	6. sibyl	11. vizier	16. catamaran
2. protean	7. perspiry	12. fuselage	17. fanfaronade
3. rickets	8. judgeship	13. cozen	18. autarky
4. ricketiness	9. judgmatic	14. gelatinous	19. manacles
5. miscegenation	10. androgyny	15. shoo-in	20. foreordain

THREE-WORD QUIZZICLES 71–75, PAGE 158

Seventy-one	1. purlieu	2. vindaloo	3. quipu
Seventy-two	1. clavichord	2. autoclave	3. clavicle
Seventy-three	1. immanent	2. emollient	3. emolument
Seventy-four	1. dinginess	2. dengue	3. dinghies
Seventy-five	1. armillary	2. emissary	3. lamasary

-ER OR -OR 1, PAGE 160

1. estimator	8. discriminator	15. predictor	22. consummator
2. facilitator	9. forfeiter	16. perpetuator	23. proselytizer
3. hallucinator	10. extirpator	17. enumerator	24. improvisator
4. mutilator	11. depredator	18. cultivator	25. arbiter
5. repudiator	12. placater	19. accumulator	
6. infector	13. inculcator	20. pollinator	
7. separator	14. insinuator	21. educator	

MULTIPLE CHOICE 12, PAGE 160

1. b. hasenpfeffer, hassenpfeffer	6. c. innards	12. a. aperitif	18. c. Kriss Kringle
	7. b. opalescent	13. d. compos mentis	19. c. hermeneutics
2. b. loupe	8. b. sarsaparilla	14. b. reveille	20. a. piranha, piraña
3. a. kiosk, kiosque	9. d. buccaneer	15. c. schnapps	
4. b. palette	10. b. napery	16. b. psychedelic	
5. b. coquetry	11. b. paregoric	17. d. eleemosynary	

FIVE-WORD QUIZZICLES 31–33, PAGE 162

Thirty-one	1. polyp	2. dollop	3. julep	4. tittup	5. turnip
Thirty-two	1. toupee	2. topee, topi	3. taupe	4. topi	5. topiary
Thirty-three	1. Phillipines	2. Filipino	3. Phillips	4. philippic	5. filiopietistic

SPELL FOR YOUR SUPPER, PAGE 164

Seventeen of the fifty culinary terms are incorrect. The misspelled comestibles are 2, 3, 4, 8, 10, 15, 16, 19, 20, 21, 26, 30, 36, 37, 44, 47, and 49.

The corrected spellings are blanc mange, jambalaya, fettuccelle, baguette, Valpolicella, beef bourguignon, Nesselrode pie, wasabi, Chilean sea bass, langoustine, galantine of turkey, annatto, kreplach, cannelloni, Pouilly-Fuissé, arugala, and anasazi beans.

THREE-WORD QUIZZICLES 76–80, PAGE 165

Seventy-six	1. Piscean	2. epicene	3. piscine
Seventy-seven	1. citronella	2. amygdala	3. muleta
Seventy-eight	1. fuchsia	2. focaccia	3. naphtha
Seventy-nine	1. phalanstery	2. facies	3. phalanges
Eighty	1. larboard	2. blackguard	3. halberd

SAY IT AND SPELL IT 12, PAGE 167

1. mosey	6. Briton	11. bombardier	16. hennery
2. posy	7. cliquy, cliquey	12. yeses	17. riveter
3. hamadryad	8. riddance	13. ethanol	18. chicly
4. sybaritism	9. imbroglio	14. murmurer	19. cilantro
5. consanguineous	10. spininess	15. caesura	20. bouillon

-ER OR -OR 2, PAGE 169

1. abbreviator	8. dissertator	15. perpetrator	22. pontificator
2. confiscator	9. absconder	16. inveigher	23. alienator
3. sojourner	10. punctuator	17. advocator	24. denigrator
4. formulator	11. initiator	18. disburser	25. dissimulator
5. masticator	12. contester	19. illuminator	
6. subjugator	13. tergiversator	20. extrapolator	
7. obliterator	14. execrator	21. attractor	

MULTIPLE CHOICE 13, PAGE 169

1. b. senary	6. c. camellia	11. a. appoggiatura	16. d. zeppelin
2. a. ophthalmology	7. a. sibilant	12. b. maggoty	17. c. soutane
3. b. bouillabaisse	8. d. smorgasbord	13. d. chukka	18. a. tohubohu
4. b. caduceus	9. c. camaraderie	14. d. appurtenance	19. c. cirrhosis
5. b. Sheol	10. b. jitney	15. a. chapleted	20. b. scimitar

THREE-WORD QUIZZICLES 81–85, PAGE 171

Eighty-one	1. bracken	2. kraken	3. lichen
Eighty-two	1. timbre	2. temblor	3. tummler
Eighty-three	1. syrinx	2. cerumen	3. sirenian
Eighty-four	1. atoll	2. avatar	3. attar
Eighty-five	1. barbet	2. barbette	3. burbot

AMERICAN CITIES, PAGE 173

1. d. Tallahassee
2. c. Albuquerque
3. c. Ypsilanti
4. d. Wahpeton
5. d. Corvallis
6. b. Oskaloosa
7. b. Chattanooga
8. d. Schenectady
9. b. Wilkes-Barre
10. d. Chillicothe
11. c. Amarillo
12. a. Champaign
13. c. Bogalusa
14. a. Casper
15. a. Manasquan
16. c. Elkhart
17. a. Meriden
18. a. Fredericksburg
19. c. Montpelier
20. d. Savannah
21. d. Sheboygan
22. d. Missoula
23. c. Paragould
24. b. Tuscaloosa
25. a. Brainerd
26. b. Atchison
27. b. McAlester
28. d. Tooele
29. a. Petaluma
30. d. Pocatello
31. d. Spartanburg
32. a. Paducah
33. c. Vermillion
34. a. Woonsocket
35. a. Buckhannon
36. d. Chicopee
37. d. Wenatchee
38. b. Ketchikan
39. d. Wailuku
40. a. Hattiesburg
41. a. Walsenburg
42. c. Plaistow
43. d. Millinocket
44. a. Sedalia
45. b. Winnemucca
46. a. Dundalk
47. b. Smyrna
48. d. Kannapolis
49. c. Holdrege
50. c. Bisbee

SAY IT AND SPELL IT 13, PAGE 178

1. schmoes
2. puerilely
3. malaguena
4. contumelious
5. remittance
6. remittent
7. apothegm, apophthegm
8. puncheon
9. croup
10. miry
11. gesso
12. lingonberry
13. ne'er-do-well
14. ibuprofen
15. parietals
16. pyknic
17. hoyden
18. pharisaism
19. packet
20. sol-fa

FIVE-WORD QUIZZICLES 34–36, PAGE 180

Thirty-four 1. recension 2. recision 3. rescissible 4. recidivism 5. reseda
Thirty-five 1. writhing 2. tithing 3. lathing 4. seething 5. scything
Thirty-six 1. cotta 2. cotyledon 3. kata 4. khedive 5. kombu

FIELD TEST 1: SOCIAL SCIENCES, PAGE 182

1. a. Australopithecene
2. c. apotropaic
3. c. henotheism
4. b. satyagraha
5. a. Peloponnesian War
6. a. Menshevik
7. b. quadrumanous
8. b. dolichocephalic
9. c. postremogeniture
10. b. anankastic
11. a. suzerainty
12. c. aggiornamento
13. a. Olduvai Gorge
14. c. potlatch
15. c. Wechsler-Bellevue
16. c. Thermopylae
17. a. Ashkenazim
18. a. irredentism
19. a. kakistocracy
20. c. Acheulean
21. b. casus belli
22. c. eidetic
23. b. hebephrenia
24. c. anticathexis
25. b. Kemal Ataturk
26. a. ekistics
27. c. Appomattox
28. a. labret
29. b. phratry
30. c. Stakhanovite

THREE-WORD QUIZZICLES 86–90, PAGE 185

	1.	2.	3.
Eighty-six	duiker	sypher	phreaker
Eighty-seven	odeum	odium	aubade
Eighty-eight	pillion	minion	minyan
Eighty-nine	gazelle	gazetteer	lazaretto
Ninety	acrostic	catachrestic	katabatic

MULTIPLE CHOICE 14, PAGE 187

1. b. gelignite
2. c. vaqueros
3. b. daiquiri
4. d. anemometer
5. a. topsy-turviness
6. c. topsy-turvydom
7. b. luau
8. d. spinnaker
9. d. dirndl
10. a. finagle
11. b. terete
12. d. spelunker
13. b. kindergartner, kindergartener
14. a. jodhpurs
15. b. barrette
16. c. manicotti
17. d. paean
18. b. slaveys
19. a. fricassee
20. d. marquee

WORLD GEOGRAPHY, PAGE 189

1. b. Liechtenstein	**15.** b. Hokkaido	**29.** c. Guinea-Bissau	**43.** a. Kuala Lumpur
2. a. Adelaide	**16.** b. Leicestershire	**30.** c. Andaman Islands	**44.** a. Okefenokee
3. b. Machu Picchu	**17.** c. Maracaibo	**31.** b. Guadalajara	**45.** b. Tipperary
4. c. Abu Dhabi	**18.** c. Kaffeeklubben	**32.** b. Papeete	**46.** c. Matabeleland
5. a. Saskatchewan	**19.** b. Brahmaputra	**33.** c. Ellesmere Island	**47.** a. Novosibirsk
6. b. Kauai	**20.** c. Edinburgh	**34.** a. Atacama Desert	**48.** c. Moluccas
7. a. Apennines	**21.** c. Balearic	**35.** a. Dhaulagiri	**49.** b. Straits of Mackinac
8. b. Riyadh	**22.** c. Phnom Penh	**36.** a. Irawaddy	**50.** b. Bournemouth
9. c. Uppsala	**23.** b. Lake Titicaca	**37.** c. Dardanelles	
10. b. Djibouti	**24.** b. Johannesburg	**38.** c. Uttar Pradesh	
11. c. Tyrrhenian Sea	**25.** c. Berchtesgaden	**39.** c. Rawalpindi	
12. b. Reykjavik	**26.** a. Tallahatchie	**40.** a. Sea of Okhotsk	
13. b. Kyrgyzstan	**27.** b. Chattahoochee	**41.** c. Eleuthera	
14. b. Sault Sainte Marie	**28.** c. Montevideo	**42.** c. Amundsen Sea	

SAY IT AND SPELL IT 14, PAGE 193

1. bouillabaisse	**6.** abetment	**11.** pollywog, polliwog	**16.** sinfonietta
2. bibelot	**7.** flivver	**12.** Decalogue	**17.** inure
3. keloid	**8.** bismuth	**13.** celadon	**18.** entr'acte
4. autochthonous	**9.** Cyrillic	**14.** coevality	**19.** septuagenarian
5. perigee	**10.** flocculent	**15.** dishabille, deshabille	**20.** juju

THREE-WORD QUIZZICLES 91–95, PAGE 196

Ninety-one	**1.** rhonchus	**2.** cheongsam	**3.** khamsin
Ninety-two	**1.** acedia	**2.** aporia	**3.** acetylsalicylic (acid)
Ninety-three	**1.** élan vital	**2.** femme fatale	**3.** kraal
Ninety-four	**1.** esker	**2.** eschar	**3.** gypper
Ninety-five	**1.** bobolink	**2.** babka	**3.** bobbin

FIELD TEST 2: FINE ARTS, PAGE 198

1. a. pleinairism
2. c. de Stijl
3. c. churrigueresque
4. b. seicento
5. c. sfumato
6. a. grisaille
7. a. entasis
8. a. kouros
9. b. Phidias
10. c. contrapposto
11. b. tenebrism
12. c. Hokusai
13. c. Mesopotamian
14. a. uraeus
15. c. tympanum
16. b. cloisonnée
17. a. corbel
18. b. corbeil
19. c. Praxiteles
20. c. Terbrugghen
21. c. plateresque
22. b. Pissarro
23. a. Caravaggio
24. a. stele
25. a. stylobate
26. c. galilee
27. b. eurythmy
28. b. Botticelli
29. b. xylography
30. a. triptych

MULTIPLE CHOICE 15, PAGE 200

1. c. odysseys
2. c. shillelagh, shillalah
3. a. whippoorwill
4. c. vichyssoise
5. d. pari-mutuel
6. d. sassafras
7. d. florilegium
8. b. castanets
9. d. diocesan
10. a. reredos
11. a. granary
12. c. hullabaloo, hullaballoo
13. c. kewpie
14. b. millennium
15. c. bialys
16. b. obeisance
17. b. Weimaraner
18. d. tinselry
19. c. simoleon
20. d. babushka

FIVE-WORD QUIZZICLES 37–39, PAGE 203

Thirty-seven 1. teratology 2. terrarium 3. toreutics 4. terreplein 5. pteradology
Thirty-eight 1. cerements 2. serotonin 3. cinerarium 4. seraglio 5. cenote
Thirty-nine 1. hiatal 2. halal 3. hiemal 4. hyetal 5. halcyon

FLUSTER CLUSTER 3, PAGE 205

There are six misspellings in the passage: rotourier, estominet, assaying, Toquay, strathspay, and animé. The correct spellings for these words are roturier, estaminet, essaying, Tokay, strathspey, and anime.

FIELD TEST 3: NATURAL SCIENCES, PAGE 205

1. c. aphelion
2. a. oersted
3. c. aurora borealis
4. b. barretter
5. b. micaceous
6. c. beryllium
7. c. gabbroic
8. b. selenodesy
9. b. saprophyte
10. c. coenocyte

11. c. bremsstrahlung
12. c. ecesis
13. a. karyogamy
14. c. Van de Graaff generator
15. b. technetium
16. c. Boötes
17. b. Becquerel
18. b. syzygy
19. c. Cepheid
20. c. scolex

21. a. poise
22. a. dicotyledon
23. b. arylate
24. c. thixotropy
25. c. stoichiometry
26. b. quaquaversal
27. b. enthalpy
28. a. Pleistocene
29. b. Mitscherlich's law
30. c. lyophize

THREE-WORD QUIZZICLES 96–100, PAGE 208

	1.	2.	3.
Ninety-six	nacelle	philomel	morel
Ninety-seven	enervate	anaphora	innervate
Ninety-eight	amaretto	inamorato	amoretto
Ninety-nine	effendi	Afrikaner	amandine
One Hundred	solar plexus	anaphylaxis	tmesis

SAY IT AND SPELL IT 15, PAGE 210

1. cirrocumulus
2. onomatopoeia
3. fluxion
4. poultice
5. annular
6. jim-dandy
7. fussbudgety
8. madrilene
9. legerdemain
10. ocarina
11. funicular
12. hallelujah
13. alleluia
14. papyrus
15. dissertator
16. putrescible
17. euchre
18. Noachian
19. potsherd
20. recusancy

FIELD TEST 4: PERFORMING ARTS, PAGE 212

1. b. Anouilh
2. c. fioritura
3. b. labanotation
4. a. cabaletta
5. a. mixolydian
6. a. Aeschylus
7. c. entrechat
8. b. Khachaturian
9. c. dodecaphony
10. b. passacaglia
11. a. neume
12. a. hamartia
13. c. cembalo
14. b. rallentando
15. a. tessitura
16. a. zapateado
17. b. *Così fan tutte*
18. c. melodeon
19. c. melismatic
20. c. Messiaen
21. c. sforzando
22. c. sfogato
23. b. Grand Guignol
24. c. denouement
25. c. Bösendorfer
26. c. Diaghilev
27. c. coloratura
28. c. descant
29. b. Köchel listing
30. c. Gesamtkunstwerk

SCRABBLEY JUMBLE, PAGE 215

1. smaragd
2. lacertilian
3. banausic
4. frisson
5. chryselephantine
6. siccative
7. chilblain
8. saxicolous
9. maillot
10. duumvirate
11. chalcotrypt
12. thaumaturge
13. vicissitudinous
14. wassailed
15. virescence
16. eschatology
17. instauration
18. tarentella
19. logodaedaly
20. samizdat

THREE-WORD QUIZZICLES 101–105, PAGE 217

One Hundred One	1. canonic	2. chthonic	3. messianic
One Hundred Two	1. mimicry	2. gimmickry	3. statically
One Hundred Three	1. theremin	2. Immelmann	3. telamon
One Hundred Four	1. aphasia	2. affenpinscher	3. officinal
One Hundred Five	1. caret	2. carotid	3. carroty

-ABLE OR -IBLE 1, PAGE 219

1. amassable
2. analyzable
3. appeasable
4. biddable
5. codable
6. committable
7. compassable
8. condemnable
9. contestable
10. corrodible
11. corruptible
12. definable
13. degradable
14. deterrable
15. dispensable
16. erectable
17. excerptible
18. exhaustible
19. expandable
20. gaugeable
21. gelable
22. imputable
23. indelible
24. indubitable
25. ingestible

-ABLE OR -IBLE 2, PAGE 220

1. interruptible
2. kissable
3. leasable
4. limitable
5. locatable
6. measurable
7. partible
8. persuadable
9. pleasable
10. ponderable
11. postponable
12. producible
13. refutable
14. remittable
15. resistible
16. salvageable
17. scalable
18. scannable
19. spareable
20. submergible
21. tithable
22. unbudgeable
23. unimpeachable
24. vanquishable
25. winnable

FIVE-WORD QUIZZICLES 40–42, PAGE 221

Forty   1. palladium   2. paladin   3. pelota   4. palinode   5. pallet
Forty-one   1. ileum   2. Ilium   3. ilium   4. ullage   5. ylem
Forty-two   1. cannoli   2. Capella   3. canola   4. kerygma   5. Kannada

-ABLE OR -IBLE 3, PAGE 223

1. suppressible
2. addressable
3. confessable
4. compressible
5. fusible
6. excusable
7. infusible
8. confusable
9. defensible
10. defendable
11. censurable
12. censorable
13. reversible
14. traversable
15. invertible
16. deductible
17. conductible
18. comprehendible
19. comprehensible
20. contractible
21. intractable
22. delectable
23. dissectible
24. effectible
25. rejectable

KILLER BEE 1, PAGE 223

1. phycology
2. filariasis
3. felucca
4. phillumenist
5. phlogiston
6. philhellene
7. phyletic
8. phasmid
9. fuligenous
10. phalarope

KILLER BEE 2, PAGE 224

1. paradiddle
2. periapt
3. paronomastic
4. paronymous
5. pyriform
6. Pyrrhonist
7. pyrosis
8. pari passu
9. parquetry
10. parosmia

KILLER BEE 3, PAGE 225

1. troche
2. newbie
3. systole
4. chamois
5. schipperke
6. trochee
7. Ate
8. bacchante
9. torii
10. étui

KILLER BEE 4, PAGE 226

1. Kwakiutl
2. quadraphonic
3. quondam
4. Quonset
5. cuadrilla
6. quokka
7. quodlibet
8. kwashiorkor
9. quinquennium
10. quadrisyllabic

KILLER BEE 5, PAGE 227

1. sorosis
2. psilosis
3. psorosis
4. psoriasis
5. sorosis
6. siriasis
7. cereus
8. psittacosis
9. cysticercosis
10. Sirius

A Brief Early History of the Spelling Bee

For many Americans, the spelling bee is no mere rote schoolroom exercise. It is a sort of institution, socially as well as educationally, as the late linguistic scholar Allen Walker Read has certified in his researches into the subject (and to whom we are greatly indebted here). Mr. Read was, among other things, the world's foremost authority on the all-American term OK (or *okay*).

Spelling bees, Read notes in an article written for the Modern Language Association, "take rank among the conservative influences in American speech. They are a factor that helps to account for the prevalence of spelling pronunciations [careful, syllabic pronunciations of words based on the written rather than the heard word] in the United States and for a central body of speech that does not yield to passing fashions."

Many educators today see little point in old-fashioned oral spelling exercises. They feel that having pupils vocalize letters ("w-o-r-d") detracts from the more important matter of the sounds that those letters represent, and insist that we properly use spelling for writing, not for pronouncing aloud. But others argue that while the spelling bee seems only a competitive exercise in alphabetic recall, there's no getting away from another fact: It motivates children—and adults, for that matter—to improve their spelling.

Bees have been in and out of fashion over the years since the first "trials in spelling" musters were held in American schoolrooms in the late eighteenth century. Such "matches" or "schools" or "spell-downs"—they were not commonly called bees until about 1875—were an established practice before the American Revolution. We owe the British some acknowledgment here, for two centuries earlier, Elizabethan schools sometimes had pupils "opposing" one another in a spelling-improvement exercise. As Read points out, it was important then, as it is today for National Spelling Bee entrants, that the pupil carefully syllabify in spelling the words aloud.

But spelling matches, except for a brief period in the late nineteenth century, never found much favor in Great Britain—although the British press often reported on the phenomenon in America (and seemed to think that "bee" referred to a single spelling contestant). Perhaps this was due to the fact that England didn't possess a Benjamin Franklin, whose urgings regarding the importance of orthography (and of dividing words into syllables) gave impetus to competitive spelling in our country. Franklin recommended pairing students off, with one giving the other ten words to be spelled each day. He was also wise enough to know that the winner should have a reward, "a pretty neat Book of some Kind useful in their future Studies."

In subsequent years, in Connecticut, Rhode Island, Maine, New Hampshire, and other states, the victor's prize was more often than not the classic act of moving ahead a place in line or to the head of the class (or row of classroom desks), or a certificate of good scholarship. For preparation, pupils used special spelling books (like those of Noah Webster, which were so enormously successful). Spell-downs, Edna Furness notes in *Spelling for the Millions*, were often a special treat on Friday afternoons that pupils looked forward to all week. Sometimes they were a reward for good performance in studies or for good conduct. "And sometimes spelling competition was 'the program' at parent-teacher get-togethers to demonstrate the teacher's ability and the pupils' progress. The spelling bees, however, were not limited to the schoolroom. At frontier functions, many a person won prestige and position in the community by spelling down the others. At a box [lunch] social the crowning event was often a spelling bee."

Bees thus became a community social occasion, with champions from different schools assembling for a showdown at a given schoolhouse or church in the evening. In New Hampshire, the astoundingly precocious Horace Greeley, later a renowned journalist and political figure, attended such matches at the age of four—and even at that age was sometimes the winner. Particularly during the first quarter of the nineteenth century, citizens flocked to these—for the time—almost glamorous events. American pupils discovered the giddy thrill and pride of accomplishment in spelling down a rival classmate or challenger from another school or area.

Great passions could be—and still are—aroused in the conducting of spelling bees. Evidently, officiating schoolmasters were sometimes less than fair to the contestants, especially when spellers were in top form, things were running late, and a loser had to be found. Read cites an 1832 diary of a Maine woman teaching in Indiana who reported how the spelling-master would use trickery when desperate:

" 'Bay' will perhaps be the sound; one scholar spells it 'bey,' another 'bay,' while the master all the times means 'ba,' which comes within the rule, being *in the spelling book*."

Edward Eggleston's 1871 novel called *The Hoosier Schoolmaster*, which did much to popularize bees in the Frontier West, had the super-spelling hero meet defeat only when Squire Hawkins pulled out of his pocket "a list of words just coming into use in those days—words not in the spelling-book"; and the hero was unable to spell *daguerreotype*. More often than not, too, we might remember, words given to pupils to spell were not defined or explained back then.

When spelling bees fell out of fashion or became too "social" in the somewhat puritanical East, they went—with frontier-minded schoolteachers—west, to Illinois, Iowa, Indiana, even California, where they became esteemed as "cultural" events. But spelling bees were too much a part of culture in the East to be completely forgotten there, and it was in Philadelphia, on March 25, 1875, that the bee of all bees was held. Eighty competitors looked word after word in the eye before an unruly crowd of some four thousand people at the grand Academy of Music. (The words that defeated five of the final six contestants were *purview*, *testacious* [sic], *distension*, *infinitessimal* [sic], and (misspelled by the runner-up) *hauser* [sic]. Two months later, a match staged at a Hartford, Connecticut, church was introduced by none other than Mark Twain, who had his inimitable doubts about the sanity of the occasion (see page 266).

The spelling bee did not remain quite so fashionable, though it never left the American schoolroom for good. Bees languished in the early 1900s, then enjoyed a revival in the 1920s and 1930s, when for a while they became features on radio programs.

Today bees are not quite the folksy communal events they once were. But for many Americans the spelling bee is an indispensable part of our national cultural heritage. In our grade schools, as part of a lengthy and carefully regulated process leading to a national scholastic title, spelling bees have become highly competitive. The Scripps National Spelling Bee finals are now a prime-time event on television, and each year a single, remarkable American schoolgirl or schoolboy is crowned as America's orthographic titleholder. (For an excellent and lively history of the National Spelling Bee over recent years, see James Maguire's *American Bee*.) In recent years an interest in bees has spread to Americans of all ages, and adult spelling competitions—from bars to boardrooms—are taking root all over the United States.

Mark Twain's Introduction to a Spelling Bee

(The following introductory remarks were tendered by Mark Twain in Hartford, Connecticut, in 1875, as a prelude to a spelling bee held at the Asylum Hill Congregational Church. We owe their preservation to the fact that they happened to be taken down stenographically.)

Ladies and Gentlemen: I have been honored with the office of introducing these approaching orthographical solemnities with a few remarks.

The temperance crusade swept the land some time ago—that is, that vast portion of the land where it was needed—but it skipped Hartford. Now comes this new spelling epidemic, and this time *we* are stricken. So I suppose we needed the affliction. I don't say we needed it, for I don't see any use in spelling a word right, and never did. I mean I don't see any use in having a uniform and arbitrary way of spelling words. We might as well make all clothes alike and cook all dishes alike. Sameness is tiresome, variety is pleasing.

I have a correspondent whose letters are always a refreshment to me; there is such a breezy, unfettered originality about his orthography. He always spells Kow with a large K. Now that is just as good as to spell it with a small one. It is better. It gives the imagination a broader field, a wider scope. It suggests to the mind a grand, vague, impressive, new kind of cow. Supurb effects can be produced by variegated spelling.

Now, there is Blind Tom, the musical prodigy. He always spells a word according to the sound that is carried to his ear. And he is an enthusiast in orthography. When you give him a word he shouts it out—puts all his soul into it. I once heard him called up to spell orang-outang before an audience. He said, "O, r-a-n-g, orang, g-e-r, ger oranger, t-a-n-g, tang, orranggertang!"

Now, a body can respect an orang-outang that spells his name in a vigorous way like that. But the feeble dictionary makes a mere kitten of him.

In the old times people spelled just as they pleased. That was the right idea. You had two chances at a stranger then. You knew a strong man from a weak one by his iron-clad spelling, and his handwriting helped you to verify your verdict.

Some people have an idea that correct spelling can be taught, and taught to anybody. That is a mistake. The spelling faculty is born in man, like poetry, music and art. It is a gift; it is a talent. People who have this gift in a high degree need only to see a word once in print and it is forever photographed upon their memory. They cannot forget it. People who haven't it must be content to spell more or less like—like thunder—and expect to splinter the dictionary wherever their orthographical lightning happens to strike.

There are 114,000 words in the unabridged dictionary. I know a lady who can spell only 180 of them right. She steers clear of all the rest. She can't learn any more. So her letters always consist of those constantly-recurring 180 words. Now and then, when she finds herself obliged to write upon a subject which necessitates the use of some other words, she—well, she don't write on that subject.

I have a relative in New York who is almost sublimely gifted. She can't spell any word right. There is a game called Verbarium. A dozen people are each provided with a sheet of paper, across the top of which is written a long word like kaleidoscopical, or something like that, and the game is to see who can make up the most words out of that in three minutes, always beginning with the initial letter of the word. Upon one occasion the word was cofferdam. When time was called everybody had built from five to twenty words except this young lady. She had only one word—calf. We all studied a moment and then said: "Why, there is no 'l' in cofferdam!" Then we examined her paper. To the eternal honor of that inspired, unconscious, sublimely independent soul be it said, she had spelled the word 'caff'! If anybody here can spell calf any more sensibly than that let him step to the front and take his milk.

The insurrection will now begin.

Planning a Bee—Some Tips

Do you envision a spelling bee—one you could organize, at a venue you'd select, with people of your choosing to compete in, and for which you'd get to make up that secret list of challenging spelling words? (This makes you a Wanna-Bee in the very best sense of that term.)

If you haven't already participated in one, you should know that adult or grown-up spelling bees—weekly, monthly, annual, or only occasional—have been flourishing in cities and towns across the United States in recent years. Today spelling bees are no longer associated only with primary education and precocious grade-schoolers.

They don't have to be staged in classrooms or school auditoriums or corporate workplaces. They don't require numerous elimination rounds. They needn't be regional in scope or be expensive to stage.

Your bee, of course, can be a modest event. One with some informality and all-in-good-fun humor in the air. A bee that you can hold at your home, in your backyard, or at your nearby community or senior center.

Among the reasons (or excuses) to hold a bee:

- social (a why-not impulse, a way to entertain friends, at a dinner party, say)
- charitable (to raise money for a cause)
- celebratory (to honor somebody's achievement, retirement, birthday, anniversary, etc.)
- promotional (to create buzz or attract potential customers to your café, bar, or bookstore, for example)

Here are a few things worth keeping in mind:

Depending on its scope, you'll probably need some help with preparations and with getting the word out. You'll need a host or pronouncer and judge or judges. And whom will you designate for that plum job—the prompt ringer of the little desk bell when a contestant misspells the word? Is there a local celebrity you'd like to involve in your bee in some way?

A few particular matters to think about:

- Will people compete individually or in teams?
- Keep in mind your venue needs to be able to accommodate all participants and spectators.
- How will you publicize the bee (assuming it's open to the public)? Do you have in mind a catchy or colorful name for your bee?
- What are your budget limitations?

Procedural or competition details to consider:

- Who will compile the list of words for the bee?
- What dictionary or other sources will be used?
- How hard do you want the words to be? Do you want them to vary in difficulty?
- Will the words be read aloud in a predetermined order? Should the words become progressively difficult? Or (using a random approach) should competitors each time pick their words out of a hat?
- Do you want to include for all words (as in a formal bee) sentence examples, alternate pronunciations if they exist, brief information regarding each word's language of origin?
- Is this to be a standard "miss-and-out" bee—one mistake and you're toast?
- Will the contestants spell out their answers aloud? Or (more low-key) will they write their answers on a slate or card?
- Will there be a time limit for each answer?
- Will the winner receive a trophy, plaque, or other prize?

On-line, of course, you'll find myriad adult spelling bee websites to peruse for information or inspiration.

The best-known bee in America is, of course, the Scripps National Spelling Bee, a competition for schoolchildren. While your spelling bee may be for adults, the information you get from the SNSB website (www.spellingbee.com) should be helpful. In addition, the site provides hundreds of words, used in past competitions, for you to choose from should you want to.

It only remains for us to say that we hope your pencil-wielding (or -chewing) adventures through these pages have not only been fun but have also sharpened your appreciation of the literatim (or letter-for-letter) demands and aberrations of our magnificent but orthographically untamable English language. If you're already or soon to be an eager, active competitor in a local spelling bee, here's wishing you many magic spells!

Acknowledgments

We thank our agents, Jim Trupin and Liz Trupin-Pulli: Jim, for connecting us with Perigee and (not at all incidentally to us) his diverting emails; and Liz, for her sensible and always gracious advice.

We're indebted to our editor, Meg Leder, for her enthusiasm for the book, her judicious suggestions, her patience (and giving us a bit of slack when needed), and a smooth expediting of the publishing process; and to our managing editor, Jennifer Eck, and the rest of the team at Perigee.

Both Steve Weller and Diane Giddis fielded our calls no matter the hour, and we soon were relying on Steve's gently voiced observations regarding just about anything and everything. Diane, whose caring about (and experienced caretaking of) the craft of writing goes beyond mere conscientiousness, was an invaluable "extra set of eyes," our editorial catcher in the rye.

We thank Rick Pearse and Nancy O'Donohue, our steadiest liaisons to the Mother Borough, for being not just supportive but entertainingly so (sometimes in verse)—for continually checking in and "being there" for us.

Teri Lujan's keyboarding and Rachel Beyda's secretarial assistance lightened our overload of things to be done. Under deadline pressure Gene Wisoff stepped in calculatingly—as our math consultant.

We're grateful to Sebastian Barone for his housecalls as software installer, troubleshooter, bug eradicator, and coffee bringer. We often required some food with that coffee, for which—from their top-notch prime rib to their terrific cheesecake—we thank our takeout cooking haven and staff, Oasis Diner of Flatbush Avenue.

David L. Grambs has been interested in words since his first job in New York, as a dictionary definer for *American Heritage*. He is the author of *The Describer's Dictionary* and *The Endangered English Dictionary*. **Ellen S. Levine** is a web producer and writer. She has not competed in a bee since fourth grade—yet. Both live in Brooklyn, New York.

To contact the authors, please send email to ThinkYouCan Spell@gmail.com.